RELIEF WITHOUT DRUGS

RELIEF
WITHOUT
DRUGS

The
Self-Management
of
Tension, Anxiety, and Pain

AINSLIE MEARES, M.D., D.P.M.

SOUVENIR PRESS

First published in the USA by
Doubleday & Co., New York

First British Edition published 1968 by
Souvenir Press Ltd.,
43 Great Russell Street, London WC1B 3PA

Reissued 1986
Published in paperback 1994

ISBN 0 285 62718 X (casebound)
ISBN 0 285 63224 8 (paperback)

Printed in Great Britain by
The Guernsey Press Co. Ltd, Guernsey, Channel Islands

CONTENTS

PREFACE

We are all familiar with the feelings of tension and anxiety. These feelings seem to be all too common in our hectic and complex world. Perhaps you cannot describe too well exactly what the feeling is. But I am sure you will recognize some of the symptoms I am going to describe later in detail.

Your anxiety or tension may not be very severe. Perhaps you experience it as nothing more than a kind of restlessness, or a slight nervousness in social situations or at work. Perhaps you find yourself getting a little too impatient too often. Your wife or husband, your children, your friends may complain that you are irritable and on edge—or, more likely, they don't say anything at all, but they, and you, are aware that something is wrong. Perhaps you have trouble concentrating. You start in on a piece of work, only to find your mind quickly distracted to something else. You find it difficult to complete a particular job, and the fact that you know you are not working at your best makes you all the more anxious. You may have vague feelings of fear, without knowing quite what you are afraid of. Your nervous tension may show itself in a stiff, unnatural way of walking, or in the way you speak. Perhaps you have trouble falling asleep, or sleep comes in short, unsatisfying patches.

We all feel some of these symptoms in one degree or another at some time. You may have become so used to being in this tense or anxious state that you don't even recognize it as unnatural.

Some of you may have other disturbing problems which

you don't realize are caused by a high degree of anxiety. Constipation, diarrhea, a rapidly beating heart, headache, and nervous rashes frequently have their roots in bodily and mental unease. Sexual difficulties, aggressive tendencies, and feelings of insecurity are all closely associated with an undue amount of tension and anxiety.

Whatever the cause and whatever the symptoms of your anxiety, there are various ways of dealing with it. I am going to describe to you a way of dealing with anxiety that may seem almost too simple to believe. It is, in fact, the most natural way we have to improve our mental and bodily sense of well-being. It is far removed from lengthy and costly psychiatric treatment. It requires the use of no tranquilizers or other unnatural aids. It uses a basic mechanism that each of us possesses and that each of us can develop and use with tremendously satisfying results.

My method for relieving anxiety and tension requires only that you learn how to relax your body and your mind. And you *can* learn to do this. You can learn by practicing simple relaxing mental exercises that I am going to describe for you later. These relaxing mental exercises can be done at any time and in any place. As you become increasingly able to do them successfully, you will have an increasing ability to let your body relax and your mind regress to a simpler, less distressed state. As your body and mind let go and relax, your anxiety and tension diminish, and the annoying and painful symptoms they bring disappear. My method is, in fact, the body's own natural way of coping with distress.

We are all familiar, too, with pain. A session at the dentist may be painful. Childbirth is painful. A burn or a cut brings pain. Or you may suffer from some bodily disorder that puts you in constant and extreme discomfort. The relaxing mental exercises can bring you to a state of ease in which, although the pain is not removed, you experience no hurt or distress from it.

In presenting these matters to you in this book, I attempt to deal with the problems of anxiety and pain at two quite distinct levels. On the one hand, I evaluate some of the practical psychological and physiological aspects of anxiety and pain, appealing to the critical functions of your intellect. On the other hand, I describe a technique of mental exercises which involve relaxation and regression. In presenting this technique I do not describe something for your mind to evaluate; I describe something for your mind to do. You cannot evaluate the technique critically because it involves the use of your mind in its relaxed and regressed state in which the critical faculties are largely in abeyance. You can understand the benefits of the technique only by experiencing them. Here is both the strength and the weakness of this approach—the strength because through its benefits we can influence the functioning of our minds, and the weakness because we are so accustomed to using our minds logically that we are likely to reject the other approach without giving it a fair trial.

There is one further explanation that I would like to make. The original manuscript did not include any case histories. My editors, however, suggested that some material of this nature should be added. I can see that the suggestion was a good one; an excerpt from a case history can often clarify a particular point. Accordingly I have examined my notes concerning some hundreds of patients, and selected incidents which would seem to supplement the text. In general my notes are more than adequate for my treatment of the patient. But because this approach originated in my attempts to help patients and was in no way a research project, some of the case histories are not quite as full or as clear on the particular point as I would have wished them to be. But they still, I hope, illustrate the reality of the particular method under discussion.

My techniques may all seem much too simple and at times may appear illogical. Please do not be put off by this. Remember that in its regressed state, the mind functions simply, in a way that to our rational selves may not always seem quite logical. Success depends on your being prepared to go along with me.

Ainslie Meares
45 Spring Street
Melbourne, Australia
June, 1966

TO MY MEDICAL COLLEAGUES

In the profession there is an understandable tendency to frown on books dealing with self-treatment. Because of his lack of knowledge the layman tends to misinterpret medical writing. On the one hand, the basically healthy individual is liable to imagine that he suffers from the disease described in the text; on the other hand, the really sick person may be tempted to try some home remedy, and so delay effective medical treatment until it is too late. In compiling the present volume I have been conscious of these dangers.

Anxiety and pain are of universal occurrence. Yet we, as doctors, are doing little to educate people in the management of these problems. Under our medical guidance people in our culture have learned to turn too quickly to the sedative or analgesic when confronted with even minor anxiety or pain. I believe we have been wrong in this. We have failed to show people that within their bodies are natural mechanisms which they can learn to use to control the discomfort of anxiety and pain.

My book is written for the layman. You as a doctor may find it repetitive. It is intentionally so, for I have found that a certain amount of repetition is an aid in communicating these ideas. My method does not involve a wholly logical process. It is based on the mental regression which accompanies the relaxing exercises; and in this regressed state the mind works rather differently.

As a doctor, you may wonder why I have not clarified the relationship of the regressed state of mind that accompanies the relaxing exercises to hypnosis or more accurately, autohypnosis. My answer is that such a discussion would be largely academic, and would only tend to confuse the layman. Should you desire further information on this interesting point, however, I would refer you to my two books, *A System of Medical Hypnosis*, 1960 and *The Management of the Anxious Patient*, 1963, both published by W. B. Saunders; and to two papers, "What Makes the Patient Better," *Lancet*, June 10, 1961, and "What Makes the Patient Better—Atavistic Regression as a Basic Factor," *Lancet*, January 20, 1962.

Fashions come and go in medicine. In psychiatry we have just lived through an era of, "We must go to the cause of this anxiety. We must go back to the conflicts of childhood and infancy." I myself have been a party to it, and in my enthusiasm have written three books, each dealing with different techniques to uncover the forgotten conflicts of the past. They are in fact effective techniques, and patients treated by them improved; but I now know that other psychological mechanisms were operating in my relationship with the patients which were not recognized by me at the time. If there were any proof needed, those who practice behavior therapy have given it to us—patients can be led back to normal psychological health without eliciting the actual factors that brought about the condition. We as doctors should not let patients think, as they very often do, that this approach is in some way inferior to the uncovering techniques of psychoanalysis. As the method described in this book is nothing more than an activation of the normal biological process of restoration inherent in all of us, it is in fact the approach par excellence.

The book is written in the way that I speak to patients, so now I speak to you as I have to other medical doctors. When a doctor has proof that some new technique is effective, I believe he has an obligation to publicize it, even if it appears to run counter to some of the accepted medical tenets of the day. I am publishing this book because the effectiveness of my approach in alleviating anxiety and pain is beyond doubt.

The only problem that is open to question is how best to lead the individual to accept such an approach when he has in fact been indirectly conditioned against it since childhood. As doctors we like to have medical ideas presented to us objectively and with adequately controlled clinical trials to substantiate the claims being made. The present work does not lend itself to such an approach. The ideas themselves are not presented objectively and I have not tried to do so. In fact I have done all I can to bring the reader simply to believe and accept my ideas in the hope that this will lead him to the little patience and self-discipline the method requires. I make no apology for being forthright when the occasion demands it, and I say this in particular reference to the ideas expressed on the treatment of bronchial asthma. I have had some doubts about the propriety of including excerpts from case histories. One's colleagues are inclined to frown on the publication of successful cases in anything but a medical journal. I think this attitude is probably stronger in Australia than in America. I am so convinced, however, my system of treatment is valuable, that if the layman finds it easier to go along with me when he reads of the successful treatment of cases like his own, that is justification enough.

Many millions of people throughout the world suffer from mild degrees of tension and anxiety. Only a few of them will ever see a psychiatrist, and those who do are sometimes not helped very much. Far too often we hear the expression, "You must learn to live with it." This is not good enough. Better to be able to say in all truth, "Do this, and you will come to live without it." I hope you will give these people the little encouragement which is so important to anyone as he starts on a new venture that at first seems almost too big for him.

INTRODUCTION

As you pick up this book you immediately ask yourself, "Is the man who writes this free of all tension and pain himself?"

No. I admit it quite openly. I am not completely free of tension and pain. But on the other hand, the general level of my tension is so much less, and my tolerance of pain so increased since commencing this study, that I feel an urgent need to communicate this experience, so that you too may share in this greater ease of body and mind.

My most difficult task is bringing you to understand that the relief of tension and pain can be a relatively simple procedure which anyone can learn if he goes about it in the right way. There is no doubt about this. The evidence for it is my personal experience in experiments I have carried out on myself and the testimony of hundreds of patients whom I have taught the procedures that I am about to describe. I state this quite categorically, as the main obstacle in the relief of tension and pain is the sufferer's belief that he can do nothing about it, save take increasing doses of sedatives, tranquilizers, and pain-killing drugs. The first hurdle, then, is the feeling that nothing can be done.

We tend to believe a person more readily when we know something about him. So I feel I must tell you something of myself and the experience on which this work is based. It will then be easier for you to believe me when I tell you that we can learn to modify our experience of nervous tension and pain by the act of our minds; and that this is a relatively simple process which can be mastered by almost anyone who is prepared to devote a little time and patience to the matter.

I am a psychiatrist, and over the years I have used all the orthodox forms of treatment to help my patients. I have found hypnosis much more effective than the usual forms of psychotherapy which aim to bring to light childhood conflicts and relate them to present problems. My experience has been that the patient often still retained his symptoms even when the childhood conflicts had been brought to the surface and he appeared to have full understanding of the cause of his condition. My results with hypnosis have been much more satisfactory. My work in this field led me into contact with others in different countries, and a few years ago I was honored to become President of the International Society for Clinical and Experimental Hypnosis.

By the use of hypnosis I was able to relieve many patients of pain which was of psychological origin; however, I soon found myself helping a number of patients whose pain was not due to psychological causes but rather to organic disease. At this stage the thought came to me that many Eastern mystics, particularly the yogis of India, are credited with having such control over their bodies that they are practically immune to pain. So I set off in search of yogis in the hope that I could find something in their methods that could be used in the consulting-room psychiatry of the Western world.

I visted Burma, India, and Kashmir, conferring with various yogis and wise men without any very startling results. I then went to Nepal, and in the foothills of the Himalayas near Katmandu I had the great good fortune to find a wise man, half saint, half yogi, who was locally known as the Siva-Puri Baba. This man, who was reputed to be 134 years old, had about him such an air of serenity that one was immediately aware of his presence. He could speak perfect English, and each morning I sat with him in the forest and we talked together on the subject of my search. In response to my questioning he told me that he never experienced the sensation of tension or anxiety.

I then asked him, "Do you feel pain?"

"Yes, I feel pain." Then after a pause, he added, "But there is no hurt in it." When I questioned him further, he went on to explain that if he trod on a tack he would be aware of it, but it would not hurt him. There would be no pain in the ordinary sense.

He had achieved this state of mind through many years of meditation and ascetic practices, so I kept bringing our conversation back to the nature of meditation, which seemed to me central to the problem. One day when I had been pursuing the subject rather relentlessly, he told me, "You can show a child a banana, but you cannot tell him how it tastes." But I believe I learned enough to understand that autohypnosis plays a very important part in the meditative process. As with his analogy about the banana, the way to understand the relaxing mental exercises which I shall describe to you is by actually practicing them.

A year or so later I visted the Indonesian island of Bali, and was able to examine a fire dancer as he danced in a deep trance amid a mass of red-hot burning coconut husks. Immediately after he stopped dancing I examined his legs and spoke to him through an interpreter. To my surprise I learned that he had had no long period of training for such a feat, but had merely been selected for the task by the members of his village and had been given protection by the priest in a simple ritualistic ceremony which I had witnessed just prior to his plunging into the fire. The old man of Katmandu had spent more than a hundred years of arduous religious practice to gain his present state of mind, but this man had achieved an extraordinary defense against pain in a matter of a few moments. It occurred to me that this kind of immunity may not be so difficult to attain as one is accustomed to believe.

I began to experiment on myself. I tried sitting or lying

on a stone wall in my garden for half an hour at a time on weekends. Instead of keeping my mind on the nature of Brahma as did the old man of Katmandu, I merely concentrated on the sensations of calm and ease. While doing this I would become relatively immune to the minor discomfort of lying or sitting on the hard stone surface; and I soon noticed that the feeling of calm and ease which I had consciously induced began to stay with me during the rest of the day. I found that while in this relaxed state I could become quite oblivious of such things as pebbles under my back, and I could pierce my skin with a needle without discomfort.

Then the big chance came. I had to have a decayed tooth extracted. My usual dentist referred me to a dental surgeon, but instead I approached a dentist friend and asked him if he would co-operate with me in an experiment and take out my tooth without any anesthetic. With some insistence on my part he finally agreed, but said he must first take an X ray. The next day he phoned me saying that the X ray showed it would be a difficult extraction and that he was not prepared to proceed with the experiment. After further discussion, though, he agreed to try it. I relaxed in the dental chair, and the tooth was extracted without discomfort. I was surprised at the ease and effectiveness of the way in which pain was inhibited; and the dentist himself was truly amazed. He told me that he had had to cut the gum and peel it off the bone, then chisel away the bone to the level of the end of the root, and then extract the tooth obliquely. The dentist was so impressed that he reported our little experiment in the *Medical Journal of Australia.**

Since then I have had another tooth extracted under similar circumstances except that I had a medical colleague with me to act as observer and record my pulse rate and blood

* McCay, A. R., D.D.S., "Dental Extraction Under Self Hypnosis," *Medical Journal of Australia,* June 1, 1963.

pressure at the time of the extraction. More recently I had a sebaceous cyst removed from the back of my neck, without anesthetic and without discomfort. An interesting sidelight of this last experiment was that a week later, when about to have the stitches removed, I did not think to relax and experienced quite sharp pain when the adhesive dressing was removed from the wound.

Of course it is common practice for psychiatrists to relieve patients of pain which is of psychological origin. But now with the certainty of this knowledge derived from my own experience that organically determined pain can be influenced by act of will I proceeded to help patients whose pain was clearly organic and not psychological in origin. A number of such patients whose pain had not been relieved by large doses of analgesics have been taught in this way to control their pain. I am convinced by these successes that the ability to inhibit pain is not just some peculiar aspect of my own personality, as some of my colleagues have suggested; but it is in fact an ability latent in us all, which can be quite readily evoked with a little practice and a little patience.

This then is the background upon which this work is based: a wide experience of orthodox psychiatry and hypnosis, and firsthand contact with Eastern mystics. Then came a period of personal experimentation, followed by the relief of patients by personal instruction in the consulting room; and now this is the final step—the assistance of others in their homes through communication by the written word.

WARNING

Before going further I must give you a clear and unequivocal warning. Pain fulfills a biologically important function. It serves as a signal that all is not well with our body, and thus calls us to remove ourselves from the injurious influence, or to rest and take some remedial action for the injured or ailing part. Without the signal of pain we would simply continue on our way, and damaged or inflamed tissues would be subject to further injury. It is therefore very important that we do not abolish the sensation of pain in any part of our body unless we first find out exactly what is causing the pain. For instance, by the techniques which I am about to describe it may well be possible for you to abolish or at least reduce a pain in the lower right side of the abdomen. Such a pain may be due to acute appendicitis, and the relief of the pain by act of will might lead to dangerous consequences by delaying an operation. Similarly, headaches are usually caused by nervous upset and can safely be relieved by these techniques, but occasionally headaches are due to a cerebral tumor, which, of course, requires operative intervention. So it is important that before we relieve any pain we should be quite clear about what is actually causing the pain. Fortunately, in the great majority of cases this is obvious enough, but if there is any doubt it is important for you first to consult your doctor.

A major problem lies in the fact that the sensation of pain is very often quite unnecessarily severe; pain of much less intensity would act as a sufficient warning signal that

all is not well. In these circumstances our warning signal—
the pain—becomes an injuring influence itself. In other cases
pain persists for an unnecessarily long period. We have received the message that all is not well, and the persistence
of the pain only makes things worse. This happens quite
commonly. We see it after injury and in many chronic
conditions. In these cases relief of the pain not only saves
the individual suffering, but actually hastens the reparative
process by conserving the patient's strength.

The biological significance of nervous tension is not so
obvious as that of pain. It is a manifestation of anxiety, and
the feeling of anxiety is also a warning signal. Whereas
pain acts as a warning that all is not well with the body,
anxiety warns us that all is not well in our mind. When
we have too much to do, too many decisions to make, our
mind cannot cope with it all. We experience anxiety in the
form of nervous tension, and we are warned to do less. This
situation arises more commonly when some moral decision
is involved or when something links the present problem
with some similar experience in the past which has not
gone well for us, and which we may have completely forgotten on a conscious level.

The relief of pain saves needless suffering and hastens
the process of repair, provided that it does not delay other
appropriate treatment. The same principle applies to the relief of anxiety. Suffering is reduced, because the person
with anxiety really suffers from his mental turmoil, and the
relief of anxiety in itself helps to restore normal mental
functioning. If, however, after reasonable trial of these measures the signs of anxiety should persist, and particularly
if they are associated with feelings of depression, then you
should consult your doctor with a view to possible psychiatric treatment.

PART I

THE SELF-MANAGEMENT
OF TENSION AND ANXIETY

I

THE NATURE OF ANXIETY

If we are to learn to master our anxiety in an enlightened fashion, we must first know something of its nature. What is anxiety? Unfortunately there is no complete agreement among psychiatrists on this subject, but it is possible to make a number of general statements that help to define anxiety. The ideas which I offer you now are a summary of a theme which I have developed elsewhere.*

THE PHYSICAL BASIS OF ANXIETY

Our brain is continually receiving a great number of nervous impulses. Some of these are conscious, but the great majority are unconscious. These impulses arise from three different areas—from our external environment, from our body itself, and from our mind.

Information concerning external environment comes to our brain through our sight, hearing, smell, taste, and touch. We are aware of some of these sensations, but a great deal of information of which we are not consciously aware also comes to our brain from all parts of the body. Thus the position of our limbs is being continually reported so that we can maintain our balance. The fullness of our stomach, the mobility of our bowels, and the functioning of all our other organs are likewise continually reported.

There is an even more complex stream of impulses which arise within the brain itself. At this level are our conscious thoughts, doubts and misgivings, loves and hates. Impulses

* Ainslie Meares, *The Management of the Anxious Patient*. Philadelphia, Pennsylvania, W. B. Saunders Co., 1963.

come also from the unconscious activity of the mind. This includes all those problems and conflicts, worries and desires, which we can readily call to consciousness if we so desire. But beyond this mass of material which we can recall at will, there lies the unconscious itself with its memories of past experiences and all the hopes and fears which were associated with them. Although these unconscious memories are quite beyond our recall except under certain special circumstances, they have a continual effect on our mental functioning by virtue of impulses arising from them.

All these impulses—from the environment, from the body, and from the mind—have to be dealt with and integrated to allow the smooth working of the brain. If the number of impulses becomes too great, the brain is unable to cope with the situation. There is in fact a level for all of us at which integration of the impulses becomes incomplete, and we experience this incomplete integration of the impulses as anxiety. The feeling of nervous tension or anxiety thus serves to warn us that all is not well in our mind.

The Body's Response to Anxiety. Our body reacts to anxiety with a number of physiological responses. Our heart rate is increased, our blood pressure rises, blood is diverted from the organs to the muscles, and the pupils of our eyes are dilated. The body prepares us to meet some emergency. It is really a preparation for action—for fight or flight. This response is a biologically ancient form of reaction, which we have inherited from times past when dangers were usually in the form of some threat of physical attack. The body's physiological response is well adapted to meet such a threat.

But the warning of anxiety refers to a threat from within—all is not well in our mind. And the body's traditional response to threats is of little help in this relatively new biological situation. In fact, the beating of our heart and the tensing of our muscles for physical action only tends to increase our anxiety, because there is no outward foe on whom we can vent the physical strength which has been mobilized. In other words our body responds to anxiety according to a biologically outmoded pattern of reaction which can neither rectify the cause nor help us tolerate the discomfort of our anxiety.

The general response of the body to anxiety is modified by a physiological self-regulation device. There are many such self-regulating mechanisms in the body—for instance those which control our body temperature, water balance, and the chemical constituents of the blood. The alerting response which prepares us for action by increasing our heart rate and raising our blood pressure is mediated through the sympathetic nervous system. When this system becomes too active, a self-regulating mechanism calls the parasympathetic system into activity to balance the effect of the overactive sympathetic system. But one of the main functions of the parasympathetic is to increase the mobility of the bowels and the contraction of the bladder. So anxiety in this indirect way may come to cause diarrhea or frequent urination. This, of course, has quite the opposite effect of the primary response to anxiety, which was to mobilize our bodily resources in preparation for action.

The Mind's Response to Anxiety. When more messages are arriving than the brain can properly handle, we have anxiety. Our mental apparatus becomes keyed up in an effort to cope with the situation. There is an increase of available mental energy, and this mobilized energy of the mind provides the force which produces all the various psychological symptoms of anxiety.

In its mobilized state, the mind becomes very alert, too alert, so that all the time it seems to be searching for the cause of its own disquiet. There develops a pathological over-alertness, and as a result the mind reacts to very minor stimuli which would not normally produce any response at all. Thus a noise which would normally go unheeded

causes the anxious person to start. Then he feels irritated
and upset in the knowledge that he has overreacted to a
matter of little consequence, and his inner tension is further
increased.

This over-alertness shows itself in many ways. The individual is on the lookout all the time. He is fidgety and
cannot let himself go off guard. He cannot rest because his
mind keeps him alert even when there is no need for it. It
becomes hard to sit and watch television without getting
up from the chair to relieve the tension within him. To relax
and sit still becomes a near impossibility because all the
time he is plagued with this distressing over-alertness of the
mind.

We see, then, that this over-alertness is a natural result
of anxiety. Sometimes, however, another type of reaction
takes place so that the anxious individual is in no way
over-alert, but on the contrary appears to be dulled and
apathetic. This reaction may occur when the individual is
confronted with overwhelming disaster on either a national
or a personal scale. He is struck dumb. He is in a daze,
unable to think or to move. Even when some purposeful
action on his part would minimize the disaster, he still does
nothing. This is a common reaction in times of war, particularly in the civilian population. It is seen in personal
calamity as when an individual suddenly sees his home
burned or his family killed in a road accident. This reaction
is so completely different from the primary response to anxiety by over-alertness that it requires some explanation. It
comes about by the overactivity of the self-regulatory mechanisms of the body. There is a surge of anxiety with its
accompanying over-alertness, but if this were too great the
body would be overwhelmed and unable to respond effectively. To prevent this, the self-regulatory mechanisms
come into play and inhibit the anxiety reaction. It is thus
the overreaction of the inhibiting mechanism that causes

the individual to be dulled, apathetic, and unable to take effective action.

The same reaction may occur in less dramatic form. The student when confronted with an important examination usually reacts to his anxiety by being so keyed up from over-alertness that the mind is flooded with too many thoughts that are often not well related to the problem on hand. In such circumstances it is not uncommon for the opposite reaction to occur. His mind goes blank, and try as he will, relevant thoughts to the problem simply will not come. We can now understand this paradoxical reaction to anxiety as due to the overactivity of the inhibiting mechanism. In a mild chronic form, over-inhibited anxiety may make the individual tired, listless, dull, apathetic, and unable to get going in his ordinary daily tasks. Because of his lack of initiative in doing things, such a patient often complains of depression. Futhermore he may say that he feels guilty because of his inability to work; but this reaction of inhibited anxiety is distinguished from true depression in that there is no real moral self-accusation as when the conscience is offended.

The Individual's Response to Anxiety. Most people when they experience anxiety take heed of the warning and do something about it. We do a little less work and so reduce the stream of impulses to our brain, or we take a holiday and remove ourselves from conflicts that have been disturbing us, or we rest and so give our brain a chance to re-establish equilibrium, or we take sedatives and tranquilizing drugs which further aid its integration. This works well enough when the major inflow of disturbing impulses comes from outside sources, but it is generally ineffective when it arises in our unconscious mind. In these circumstances we need something more. We shall see how this can be achieved by helping our mind to sort things out in the relaxing mental exercises which we are about to discuss.

II

COMMON SIGNS OF ANXIETY

At different times we all experience nervous tension of some degree, and we are all familiar with the more obvious signs of anxiety. However, there is a multitude of ways in which anxiety may manifest itself, and some of these are of such a nature that they often mislead both patient and doctor into the belief that the trouble is due to some organic cause rather than to the disordered function of our mind.

I have seen quite a number of patients who had suffered from long-standing anxiety and nervous tension, and who had become so accustomed to their tensed-up state that they had grown to accept it as normal. Each of these consulted me on account of some bodily symptom, and when I commented on their general state of tension, they denied that they felt tense; and it was only after treatment that they realized that an easier and more relaxed way of life was possible for them. Strangely enough, one of these patients is a well-known surgeon.

The surgeon was referred to me by another doctor in the hope that I might be able to help him with a long-standing difficulty with his speech. I could see that he was a tense person, but when I asked him about it, he strongly denied that he was in any way tense, and added that everyone who knew him regarded him as particularly relaxed. His wife was with him at the time, so I asked her to lift up my arm and let it go suddenly. It flopped down with its dead weight onto the arm of my chair. I then asked her to do the same thing with the patient. When she let his arm go it remained stuck up in the air for a moment, held there by the tension in the patient's muscles. Try as he might, he could not let his arm fall naturally and relaxed.

One day after two or three sessions of the relaxing exercises, he smiled, and said, "I never really knew that I was tense like that."

Although it has not been completely cured, his speech is much improved, and he has achieved an ease in his ordinary way of life which he had not thought possible.

The signs of anxiety are elusive and may well escape even the physician who does not specialize in this aspect of medicine.

ANXIETY IN THE MIND

Apprehension. We experience anxiety in pure form as apprehension. This is a particular form of nervous tension. There is the feeling of fear, but it is an objectless fear, and at the same time as we experience it we are aware that there is nothing that should make us afraid. When we feel real fear, we can always attach our emotion to some outside object, and say that we are afraid of this or that. But because of the objectless quality of anxiety, apprehension is extremely disturbing. We simply do not know of what we are afraid. We feel that something is going to happen, but we do not know what. Something bad is about to befall us, but we cannot imagine what it might be. If the anxiety is severe, this irrational element may evoke feelings of approaching insanity, and the disquiet of our mind is still further increased.

A patient of mine, a forty-six-year-old school teacher, showed signs of this kind of severe apprehension. In spite of quite a massive physique, he had always been rather tense and jittery. Twelve months previously he had suffered

a severe allergic reaction to one of the antibiotic drugs, and
since then he had been in a terrible state.

He described his anxiety condition in these terms: "Get
vague heart attacks." "All kind of fears." "Heart thumps and
bangs." "Keep sweating." "Get very het-up." "Attacks come
on with physical effort such as moving the TV set." "It
started with pain in legs and arms." "I walk down the street
and become stricken with fear and have to return." "Keep
waiting for something to happen." "Don't want my wife to
leave me even for a short time." "In bed the sheet touched
my throat and I thought I was strangling."

In reading this, please remember that these excerpts from
my case histories nearly all concern patients who have been
referred to me by other doctors because of the severity of
their nervous symptoms. This book is intended to help patients like this, but it is also intended to help the great host
of others who suffer only in mild degree, and who in ordinary circumstances would never seek the help of a psychiatrist or even the local doctor. Consequently, these notes
about various patients whom I have seen will serve to
illustrate the point I am trying to make. But although they
may refer to conditions which you yourself have, in all
probability in your case it is in much milder form.

In less severe form, apprehension may show itself as a
vague uneasiness. The feeling is difficult to describe. We lose
our natural calm and repose. We are uneasy. We try to pass
it off, and say to ourselves that we are all right; but we know
that we are not quite right, and the strange feeling of disquiet remains, and persistently disturbs us at our work, at
home, and even in our sleep.

A fifty-year-old woman, whom I had known for most of
my life as a robust extrovert, consulted me professionally.
She said that she had felt depressed and frightened. She
could not get going with her former zest. Her most disturbing symptom was a difficulty in breathing which was as-

sociated with a feeling of panic, so that she would catch her breath and could not properly relax.

She very quickly lost her symptoms with the relaxing exercises.

Nervous Tension. There is a difference between true apprehension and the more common nervous tension. They may occur either separately or in combination. Nervous tension is a less complicated sensation and lacks the feeling of impending disaster. We feel tense in the mind, the brain, or the whole self. Relaxation seems impossible. We feel wound-up like a spring and cannot let go. There is an absence of normal mental ease, and in its place there is the feeling of being overwrought.

This nervous tension of anxiety is often accompanied by physical muscle tension. When we are anxious, our muscles are tensed, ready for the call to action which in fact never comes. The tensed muscles may become sore and tender. If this is generalized we are said to suffer from nervous rheumatism, but more often the stiffness is confined to certain muscle groups, particularly those around the neck and shoulders.

Minor degrees of nervous tension show themselves in the way we function in our everyday life. There is a lack of ease about our reactions. Even in such a simple thing as walking, the natural ease of movement is lost, our arms do not swing in the accustomed fashion and our gait has the appearance of being strained and awkward. Sometimes these symptoms of anxiety very closely resemble those of organic illness.

A woman in her early fifties had been thoroughly investigated by a competent physician, and had had psychiatric treatment with drugs and discussion of various domestic problems. She complained to me that she was tired and lethargic. She was dizzy when she stood up and would become breathless when walking up a slight hill. She said that she was wobbly on her legs so that she had difficulty in standing to do the cooking.

I thought that an organic cause for her symptoms may have been overlooked, and I referred her back for further investigation, but nothing could be found. So I started her with relaxing mental exercises, and she has made a dramatic improvement, which shows that her symptoms were in fact due to anxiety. I later discovered that her unsteadiness on standing was due to the increased nervous tension in the muscles of her legs.

Nervous tension may be seen in our manner of speech. There is a tendency to talk abruptly and too quickly. The flow of words is interrupted and the observer is aware of a loss of natural ease of communication. In simple things such as writing, our tension makes us hold the pen too tightly. Our hand starts to shake, our writing becomes jerky, and the letters lose their normal rounded outline.

There is another aspect of nervous tension which further disturbs us. We do not like other people to know that we suffer in this way. It is considered socially desirable to be relaxed and at ease. To be tense and uncomfortable is to be socially inept, and as a result we do all we can to disguise our inner tension from those around us. We try to behave in a relaxed manner, and when we are seated we assume a posture of ease in the hope that others will not guess what is going on in our mind. In this attempt to keep from the others the truth as to how we feel, we concentrate on what we are saying and on the tone of voice as we say it. We try to present a façade to them so that they will not guess our true state of mind. To keep up this façade requires more and more effort. We have to concentrate on it so much that we can only give half our attention to the matter in hand. We become aware that we are not functioning to our full ability; we become more apprehensive, and our anxiety is still further increased.

Irritability. Anxiety commonly shows itself in irritability. We react too quickly and too much to all manner of minor frustrations. We become upset by things which would not normally disturb us. We are more sensitive to noise, and are easily irritated by it. The noises at work which we had not previously noticed become a source of irritation; and at home the noise of the children brings us to distraction. We tolerate it as long as we can, then suddenly let go. We punish the child too severely, and then immediately regret it.

If someone finds fault with what we have done, we normally take the criticism in stride. But when we are anxious, we overreact to the situation; we flare up, we say what we should not say, and then regret it. The girl in the restaurant attends to us in the usual way, but because we are tensed up we feel that she is unbearably slow. The mannerisms and quirks of our friends and relatives, which we once enjoyed, now irritate us. There soon develops an atmosphere of tension in the home. Members of the family become cautious; they are restrained, and no longer laugh and joke openly for fear of triggering off this unnatural irritability. The anxious one senses that the others are acting differently toward him, he becomes still more on edge, and the cloud of misunderstanding deepens.

A young woman in her early thirties, extremely tense and aggressive, came to consultation on account of her intense irritability with her two young children. These were her exact words: "With her like she is how could I be relaxed?" "It is not as if I am completely ignorant. I have had experience with doctors and that makes me a bit doubtful."

For some years her husband had been under treatment for a peptic ulcer which I thought might easily be related to his wife's irritability.

Her state was so severe that I arranged for her admission to a hospital, but she was so irritable and aggressive that she promptly left against advice. However, she returned to me some months later, just as irritable as ever, but determined to seek help. It took her several sessions to learn to do the relaxing mental exercises. She then underwent an extraordinary change in personality; she could smile and be pleasant in a way that had not seemed possible before. She learned to cope with the children and tolerate frustration without undue irritability.

Insomnia. Poor sleep is the rule for the anxious individual. There is difficulty often aggravated by restlessness in falling asleep. It seems impossible to get comfortable, or when some position seems comfortable it lasts only for a fleeting moment, and then it is necessary to move again. We toss and turn and worry about the problems of the ensuing day. We keep waking during the night, and each time the same restless difficulty in getting to sleep is repeated. Then if sleep comes it is commonly disturbed by frightening dreams, so that we wake in a sweat with a pounding heart and the other physiological signs of anxiety. It is worth noting that as our anxiety condition improves our dreams in general take on a less worrying quality, and when we are restored to normal mental health our dreams, or what we remember of them, no longer disturb us.

Fatigue. As one would expect from the over-alertness, nervous tension, and lack of sleep, fatigue is a constant symptom of anxiety. However, there is a quality about the fatigue of anxiety which distinguishes it from the normal fatigue of a well-done day of mental and physical activity. The latter leads us to contented rest; but fatigue of anxiety is a restless, alert kind of fatigue which quite lacks the pleasant relaxing quality of normal tiredness.

Depression. It is important that we consider the matter of depression carefully. Depression may be caused through anxiety, in which case it can be relieved by the techniques which I am about to describe; on the other hand it may result from a quite different type of nervous illness which is best treated by other means. If the sense of depression is sufficiently severe to bring the feeling that life is not worth living, or if fleeting thoughts of suicide come to mind, or if the depression is accompanied by feelings that you are somehow being punished for your past sins, then it is important that you consult your doctor to be sure that you have appropriate treatment.

Nevertheless there are two types of nervous depression which can be treated in the same way as anxiety and nervous tension. When we are tense and nervous we are aware that we are not in good health, and that we are not fulfilling our duties at work and in the home with the natural ease which helps us to do a job well. As a result we feel depressed. Things look gloomy, it seems as if a cloud were over us. It is harder to smile, harder to laugh, and harder to see the funny side of things. In fact, everything seems more difficult. Jobs which we have done in the past without effort now seem to be almost too much for us. There is a general loss of interest, and things which we used to enjoy, such as the company of our friends or a visit to the theater, no longer have any appeal for us. In its place there is a tendency to shun our friends and spend our time by ourselves, perhaps sitting and brooding, perhaps just sitting with an awful inertia hanging over our heads so that we do nothing at all. When in fact we have to do something we often feel overwhelmed by the mental effort of making a start. In lesser degree the depression may show itself as a vague listlessness, a lack of energy, and a general disinclination to get going and do things. We have noted that this type of depression is the result of incapacity arising from our anxiety and nervous tension. Accordingly it is relieved as our anxiety subsides as a result of self-management.

In the depression that arises from reaction to loss or bereavement we feel a sense of destitution, loss, and aloneness. Normal people are emotionally dependent upon one another in greater or lesser degree. The loss of dependency by death or absence of a loved one produces the normal reaction of depression, similar to the way in which fear is a normal reaction to danger. The depression becomes abnormal only if it is of undue severity or of prolonged duration. Sometimes, of course, it results from loss in the more material sense in the way of fortune or livelihood. As with the depression caused by anxiety, depression of this nature can be greatly relieved by the same principles of self-management.

Lack of Concentration. Students and those whose occupation requires steady brainwork often find that their anxiety shows itself primarily in lack of concentration. They complain of an inability to study or to give full attention to the problem at hand. This of course is a common symptom at examination time. The student sits gazing at his text without reading, or alternatively he reads the same paragraph time after time without fully comprehending what it is all about. In addition to taking the general measures for the relief of anxiety which I will describe, the student can lead himself to greater self-discipline by setting himself a limited daily program of study which he must always complete. If he starts with a daily schedule within his capacity, he will find that he can steadily increase the amount of work he can handle as his ability to relax increases. With these aids and the reduction of anxiety by the relaxing mental exercises, the ability to concentrate usually soon returns.

In other cases the same inability to concentrate is noticed in reading a novel, or the daily papers, or even in following the conversation of our friends.

Difficulties with Friends. Anxiety often shows itself in difficulty in our interpersonal relations. We feel that we are no longer at ease when meeting people, strangers, and even those whom we know quite well. Oddly enough, it is usual for us to be noticeably easier in our professional and business

COMMON SIGNS OF ANXIETY

dealings with people than we are on social occasions, even when the social occasion is quite casual and of no consequence. The reason for this is that in our professional and business dealings both we and the others have something definite to do; we have an allotted role, as it were, and we know what has to be done; but small talk and polite conversation on a casual social basis is much more difficult. Tension makes us awkward. It seems hard to establish friendly communication. We tend to become self-conscious, and aware of what we are doing and saying, whereas in a healthy state of mind our conversation happens naturally and spontaneously without any great conscious control on our part. Things seem strained. Any pause in the conversation worries us. Silence becomes unbearable, so we feel we must keep talking at all cost. Because of our inner tension we lose our easy flow of thought, relevant subjects elude us, and we become aware that our conversation is mere chatter. We are prattling, jabbering; and we try to pull ourselves together to keep our tension from those about us. On other occasions there is a poverty of speech, and we are embarrassed because we cannot say anything. Our silence is caused by the overactivity of the inhibitory process making an attempt to damp down our reaction to our anxiety. But it goes too far, and we find ourselves so inhibited that we cannot say anything. A tenseness comes between us and our friends. They in turn come to sense that we are not fully at ease, and as a result they tend to behave toward us less freely and in a more guarded fashion. The social occasion which we used to enjoy becomes a kind of nightmare—something to be avoided at all costs.

Recently, I saw a lad whose main symptom was his difficulty with his friends. To be more accurate, I should say his difficulty was with those around him, as he was fast losing all his friends.

He is a nice lad, quite a gifted university student, and a

good athlete as well. But he is incredibly tense and extremely rigid in his way of thinking, so once he gets some idea in his head, whether it be good or bad, there is no shaking him from it.

His tension and irritability were so great that I could easily see that there would be no fun for young people in the company of a lad like this. His former friends had left him for the simple reason that his tension made them feel uncomfortable.

This difficulty in interpersonal relationships resulting from anxiety may come between husband and wife so that they almost become strangers to one another; with young lovers an invisible something comes between them, cutting off the free interchange of their emotion. In a similar way the anxious mother may become separated from her baby; and try as she will, she is unable to re-establish their harmony together because the infant, in animal fashion, senses her tension and reacts to it.

Restlessness. Restlessness is closely allied to both the irritability and over-alertness which we have already discussed. The anxious patient cannot sit still. He fidgets and wriggles about. He cannot settle to the task in hand; he starts one job but feels uncomfortable, leaves it and starts something else. He is less restless when there is something definite that he has to do, so he is more comfortable at work than at home. On weekends, in spite of happy relations with his family, it is common for him to wish for Monday so that he can go back to the fixed routine of work.

Sometimes people feel that they will be better if they take a holiday and have a good rest. Of course, these patients are at their worst in such circumstances because they have lost the ability to relax and take it easy. Other people with anxiety are benefited by such a holiday, but when restlessness is a feature the anxious patient only returns more tense and frustrated than ever.

A forty-seven-year-old foreman wrote for an appointment, and described his restlessness in these terms.

"I have an inability to relax, nervous tension, anxiety complex and constant apprehension. I cannot sit [without a flush of anxiety] in meetings, church, theater, dentist's chair, barber's chair, public transport or as a passenger in a motor car . . . My flush of nervous tension makes me leave whatever I am attending . . ."

Phobias and Phobic Tension. In a phobia anxiety is manifested in a different way. The patient remains reasonably at ease until confronted with the phobic situation. He then experiences discomfort which may vary from mild apprehension to uncontrollable panic. The patient develops a fear of the particular situation which causes him this distress, and for this reason the condition is known as a phobia. Common phobias are heights, being away from home, being in crowds, or being in enclosed spaces such as elevators, toilets, or railway coaches. Knives, swords, and firearms often become the objects of phobias. In a similar way people may develop an irrational fear of certain animals such as mice, cats, moths, or snakes. The sufferer is always aware that his phobia is irrational. He knows quite well that there is nothing to be afraid of in going across the street, but this does nothing at all to relieve his sense of panic as he goes out the door. More and more he tends to stay indoors so that he soon becomes housebound, not venturing forth from one month to the next.

Obsessions and Obsessional Tension. We all evolve our own particular ways of coping with tension. Some people relieve it by "blowing their top" and ventilating their emotion, and in this way they dissipate their anxiety; some develop a studied calm in their approach to things; while with others the anxiety is concentrated in one particular limb or organ, so that the rest of the body is free. Other people cope with inner tension by making sure that they have everything just right. They feel that if everything is right there can be nothing to worry about. These are the perfectionists. They like everything neat and tidy and in order. This is likely to become an obsession with them so that they become pre-occupied with it and spend much of their time checking things over time and again. In this way they are inclined to fuss over every minor detail. It soon comes about that there is no time for the really important things, for with all their attention focused on the details they lose sight of the main issues. There is a tendency for the mind to keep churning over some particular subject and be unable to make the normal transition to other subjects of thought. At the same time the need to have things just right leads to doubts about whether things are right or not. In this way the obsessive is continually in doubt, so that he becomes a constant worrier and has such difficulty in making up his mind that even trivial decisions may become a matter of great effort. He seems to see two sides to every question; and when it comes to some important matter, such as marriage or choice of occupation, he simply dithers and is unable to come to any decision.

Nevertheless, the perfectionist way of avoiding inner tension works reasonably well in some circumstances. It is effective if the person is able to live a methodical routine way of life that allows everything to be neat and tidy and in its right place. But if something happens to change this way of life so that he can no longer follow set routines, then he becomes tense and anxious because his way of preventing tension does not work in the new set of circumstances.

This was the case with a young woman whom I have recently seen. She had been a very good nurse, in fact she had been top of her year because she was so neat and thorough that she always had everything in order. She liked her work and was free of tension as she was able to avoid worry by having everything in order. However she married, and quickly had two children. In the new circumstances with two babies to care for she was no longer able to have everything around her in perfect order. She could no longer cope with her inner tensions and broke down with severe anxiety.

Another perfectionist woman was successful in running a milk bar with her husband in a country town. Then they went to live on a dairy farm, but the presence of the mud and dirt from the cows so conflicted with her perfectionistic tendencies that she broke down with severe tension and anxiety.

Stuttering. Anxiety may have an effect on stuttering. The right side of the body is controlled by the left side of the brain and vice versa. In the right-handed person the left side of the brain is dominant over the right, and as a result the right hand is given preference over the left. In those who are left-handed the right side of the brain is dominant over the left. It is believed that stuttering often develops when the dominance of the leading side of the brain is incomplete, or when a potentially left-handed child is trained to function as a right-hander. We see then that stuttering results when the messages from the brain to the organ of speech are indecisive. This indecision may be further increased by the presence of anxiety. This is shown very clearly by the fact that many quite normal people show a hesitancy in their speaking or even a mild stutter when confronted with the task of speaking in some formal situation which produces anxiety.

On the other hand, some people stutter without showing or feeling much tension or anxiety at all. As a general rule these people who stutter in the absence of anxiety do not gain much help in their speech difficulty by practicing relaxing mental exercises. However, the majority of stutterers experience considerable tension when they are speaking, and with them the reduction of the general level of anxiety by relaxing mental exercises is a great help toward establishing a pattern of easy normal speech.

ANXIETY IN THE BODY

Palpitation. One of the commonest symptoms of anxiety is the abnormal awareness of the action of our heart. Palpitation is a normal accompaniment of a response to danger. In this case the increased action of our heart serves to prepare us to meet the threat. However, as soon as the danger passes the action of our heart returns to normal and we cease to be aware of it. But when we suffer from anxiety, the unpleasant awareness of the action of our heart is often constantly with us.

Besides the persistence of the palpitation there is another factor. In our normal response to real danger our heart does in fact beat more strongly. But in the palpitation of anxiety there may be little actual overactivity of the heart, and the unpleasant awareness is due to our hypersensitivity to the normal beating of our heart rather than to overactivity of the organ.

The feeling of palpitation focuses our attention on our heart. We are all familiar with the dangers of heart attacks from coronary thrombosis. We soon come to feel that something is wrong with our heart. To reassure us our doctor takes an electrocardiogram and tells us that it shows our heart to be quite normal and that the palpitation is only due to our nervous condition. But we are not reassured. A lurking feeling remains that there is something wrong. In fact, it is hard to be reassured so long as our anxiety is still with us.

A few years ago I saw an industrial tycoon, a man of strikingly pleasant personality and such exceptional ability that in a matter of a decade he had amassed a great fortune.

But over the previous two and a half years he had suffered from pain over his heart and quite violent palpitation; and as a result was unable to enjoy the material success he had achieved.

In the manner of the real tycoon he was determined at all costs to get himself fixed up. He was not sure whether it was ten or twelve cardiologists that he had consulted in the various capital cities of Australia. He had gone to America to the most famous cardiological clinic in that country. He had been treated by a psychiatrist in America and by three psychiatrists in Australia.

"You can tell when there is something wrong with your heart, you can feel it," he asserted.

There was obviously no point in having a head-on collision with such a man, so I merely said, "Anyway, you would be more comfortable if you were more relaxed." And we went on from there.

One day about eighteen months later I was driving home, when I caught sight of him in his car. In typical style he shouted, "Never better in my life."

I must also tell you something of the other side. Last week I saw a healthy, athletic student who was becoming crippled by pain over his heart. Two leading cardiologists had assured him that his heart was perfectly normal. He was really brought to me against his wishes, by his father. He is convinced there is something wrong with his heart. He will not listen to me. He refuses to come back. Yet I am sure that if he would only do what I suggest he would soon be free of the pain.

Rejection by the patient like this does not happen often, but it is the most common cause of failure.

Pain in the Region of the Heart. Anxiety frequently produces pain in the left side of the chest which we immediately suspect to be due to some disease of the heart. However, the pain of anxiety is usually situated well to the left side in the area where we can normally feel the heart beat. On the other hand the pain from organic disease of the heart is situated more centrally, under the breast bone. Furthermore, we experience heart pain due to anxiety at any time, even lying down and resting, while organic cardiac pain is typically brought on by physical effort and stops when we rest. Organic cardiac pain also tends to radiate down the left arm in a way which does not usually occur when the pain is of functional origin.

Only a few days ago a doctor brought his twenty-two-year-old son to me. He was a big lad of fine physique and was a successful athlete. In a pleasant extrovert manner he told me that for the past five months he had had continuous pain over his heart and down his left arm. The pain had come on when he was under a lot of stress studying for exams at a time when his girl friend was also demanding his attention, and he felt he could not cope with both. He had recently seen a cardiologist who found him normal and who had suggested a visit to me.

I have mentioned that pain over the heart due to anxiety rarely extends down the left arm. This lad was convinced that there was something wrong with his heart. He is the son of a doctor; and when I questioned him, he said that he knew quite well that pain from heart disease goes down the left arm. This serves to illustrate the way in which the symptoms of anxiety can be modified by our knowledge of our body and its functions.

Nervous Dyspepsia. Discomfort in the stomach felt beneath the ribs in the upper part of the abdomen is one of the commonest signs of anxiety. The discomfort—or if it is more severe, the pain—is very similar in nature to the pain of peptic ulcer except that the pain of nervous dyspepsia tends to be associated with emotional stress whereas ulcer pain is more clearly related to food intake. A mild persistent gnawing discomfort in the upper abdomen is often a symptom of chronic anxiety. This is frequently interrupted by intervals of more acute discomfort as the sufferer is subjected to periods of greater stress. Sometimes it is expressed as a feeling of a void or emptiness in the stomach. Other people react with acute upper abdominal discomfort to any sudden anxiety. They describe it by saying, "It gets me in the stomach." It came quite suddenly, "almost as if someone kicked me there." Other people experience anxiety as a sensation of "butterflies in the stomach," or a feeling that "the stomach turns over."

Constipation. We have noted that the main reaction of the body to anxiety is one of preparation for action—the increased output of the heart, the diversion of blood to the muscles, and the liberation of glucose into the blood to provide extra energy. Of course any movement of the bowels would hamper this preparation for physical activity, so the normal response of the body to anxiety includes a dampening down of movement of the bowels. In this way a mild anxiety reaction extending over a long period may lead to chronic constipation.

A professional man in his early fifties started the relaxing mental exercises on account of mild general tension, without thought as to any possible effect on his bowel action.

He had been constipated all his life, and for the last thirty years had been given to relieving his constipation with suppositories and enemas. After a few months, with the reduction of the general level of his anxiety, he found that he had established a perfectly normal bowel action, without physical straining, for the first time in his life.

The reduction of general anxiety undoubtedly helped by allowing the normal motility of the bowel. But the patient himself lay stress on his being relaxed when actually at the toilet.

Nervous Diarrhea. The self-regulating mechanisms of the body may come into action in an attempt to restore equilibrium from the overactivity of that part of the nervous system which prepares the body for action. In these circumstances it is quite common for the self-regulating mechanisms to overcompensate as it were. When this happens there is increased motility of the bowel, and diarrhea results instead of constipation.

> A woman of thirty-four years had always been somewhat tense and was inclined to be rather fussy and perfectionistic.
> Although not unintelligent, she had always had difficulty in coping with things which better-endowed people would have been able to take in their stride. As a result she was very dependent on her husband, who was kind and considerate. On a number of occasions when under additional stress, she had suffered from bouts of severe diarrhea. She was very anxious to have a family, but on each occasion on which she had become pregnant she had had a miscarriage. Over the years she had had a great deal of psychiatric treatment—psychotherapy, all manner of drugs, and electric shock treatment.
> When she came to me, nothing would stop her diarrhea, which had started some three months after her last miscarriage. She did the relaxing mental exercises. The diarrhea soon stopped. She has become easier in herself, and better able to cope with things, but still remains the rather ineffectual woman that she is.

Jokes about loss of control due to nervous diarrhea are so common that all must be familiar with this symptom of acute anxiety. It is common enough in less acute form with soldiers when they are about to enter the battle area, or even with students when confronted with an important examination. Anxiety is also a significant factor in the chronic forms of diarrhea known as ulcerative colitis.

Frigidity. The tense or anxious woman is commonly frigid. There is a loss of both sexual desire and sexual response. There may even be a kind of negative response so that the muscles go into spasm, making intercourse difficult or impossible. On the one hand, the anxious apprehension makes the free flow of emotion impossible; and on the other hand, the muscle tension prevents physical relaxation.

It is important to remember that the anxiety which causes frigidity may arise either from sexual conflicts or from conflicts far removed from the sexual area. Thus the anxiety of a woman who fears that she may become pregnant is likely to inhibit her sexual response and she comes to be frigid. On the other hand, a similar response may result from tension arising from conflicts at work.

Everyone knows that frigidity may be caused simply by loss of affection. If a husband is jealous or suspicious by nature, and if his wife becomes frigid, he is likely to interpret her frigidity as evidence that she has taken a lover or at least is looking elsewhere. This may happen even though the frigidity is due to anxiety from quite innocent causes. Friction develops between husband and wife; there is increased tension and the frigidity is so much the worse. Fearful lest this type of situation develop, many anxious and frigid women pretend to experience those feelings which are in fact so far from them.

Impotence. The man who suffers from loss of sexual function, particularly the strong young man, suffers much more acutely than the woman with frigidity, as impotence is a serious blow to the male ego. Unlike frigidity, his failure cannot be covered up or disguised. Young men are quite prone to sexual anxiety. This is an entirely psychological reaction, and virile appearance or athletic build are no armor against it. The anxiety often arises in an early sexual experience which has been unsuccessful because of guilt. On subsequent occasions the anxiety is rekindled and the pattern of failure becomes even more firmly established. In other cases the impotence is due to anxiety which arises from nonsexual conflicts. A man who is tired and jittery from anxiety at work may lose his sexual power. There are two quite common types of reaction of the wife who is faced with this situation. Many wives taunt the husband on the loss of his virility, which of course increases the husband's anxiety and makes his impotence worse. The other reaction is one of immediate suspicion, and the husband is promptly accused of infidelity.

Asthma. A number of factors may combine to cause bronchial asthma. Of these, allergy, infection, genetic constitution, and emotional influences are the most important. However, as is often the case in the history of medicine, the last twenty or thirty years have seen an overemphasis on one of these factors at the expense of the others. There has been a remarkable preoccupation with the allergic factors of asthma. The preparation of antigens and their use in skin testing and desensitization has all the appeal of being scientific. However, this preoccupation with allergy has led to the neglect of the emotional factors, which are much more elusive and harder to appreciate as an aspect of science. But the importance of the emotional influence is beyond all doubt.

I have had a number of patients who suffered for years from classical asthma with proven sensitivity to common pollens and dusts. They ceased to have attacks of asthma after being treated by relaxing methods, even though they were still exposed to the same pollens and dusts which in the past had caused the attacks. Furthermore these patients have shown no formation of substitute symptoms, such as skin rashes, that have been reported by some authorities when hypnosis was used to stop asthma by direct suggestion. I could quote histories of a great number of patients whose asthma was either completely relieved or at least greatly improved following the practice of relaxing mental exercises.

Perhaps one of the most remarkable was a woman of forty-six who had suffered from severe asthma for thirty years. She seemed to live by repeated use of her spray. After practicing the relaxing exercises, the woman simply ceased to have attacks, and her spray was completely abandoned. I am sure that if there had been any recurrence she would have returned to me, but she has not done so.

A lad of eighteen was incapacitated by asthma. He ceased to have attacks, and I lost contact with him until a relative came to consultation a few weeks ago, and reported that the lad had remained free of asthma since seeing me five years ago.

A young married woman was extremely sensitive to house dust, and any housework always produced a severe attack. After some relaxing treatment she came to be able to dust the house in the normal way without any ill effect.

The significant finding of my work in this field is that many patients who suffer from classical bronchial asthma cease to have attacks when the general level of their anxiety is reduced. Some other patients have continued to have attacks, but they have been much less frequent and much less severe. Other patients have remained uninfluenced by this approach. Approximately one third of the patients so far treated fall into each of these three categories. It would therefore seem that anyone suffering from bronchial asthma should at least try the method of relief through the principles of self-management described later in this book. The method reduces the general level of anxiety in a way similar to the relaxing method I have used in my office treatment.

Nervous Rashes. There is a close relationship between the skin and the nervous system. In the early development of the fertilized human ovum into the embryo, adjacent cells are split off so that some will ultimately develop into the skin and others into the nerve cells of the central nervous system. When our skin is gently stroked our nerves are calmed, but when our skin is tickled our whole nervous system is convulsed. It is therefore not surprising that activity of brain cells is often reflected in the activity of the cells of the skin. In other words, emotional stresses in the mind are apt to produce nervous rashes in the skin. This is such common knowledge that it is reflected in our everyday speech when we talk of something "getting under our skin"; and we can observe emotional reactions in the skin when people blush with embarrassment, go pale with fear, or turn livid in anger. Thus the self-management of nervous rashes involves both a reduction in the general level of anxiety and a reduction of responsiveness to emotional stress.

A doctor's wife came to see me because of a nervous rash which she had had for the past two years. I showed her a little about relaxation, and as she lived in the country it was arranged that she would return to the city in a month's time for an extended visit so that I could help her further. But she wrote canceling her appointment, saying that the rash had already cleared.

She came to see me some two years later when she had a slight recurrence. The rash quickly settled down just as on the previous occasion.

Nervous Headaches and Migraine. These two different conditions are both associated with anxiety—nervous headache directly so, and migraine less directly.

The pain of nervous headache is felt on both sides of the head, and mainly in the front part of the head and behind the eyes or at the back of the head. There is often an accompanying feeling of something pressing on top of the head or of a tight band around the head. Nervous headache is the direct result of nervous tension, and if the tension is relieved by appropriate measures the tendency to headache soon vanishes.

Migraine is a different kind of headache. It is usually proceeded by some strange feeling which acts as a warning that an attack of migraine is about to develop. There are often disturbances of vision, so that sight is impaired and further disturbed by flashes of light or bright wavy lines. Then the headache itself comes on. Unlike nervous headache, migraine is usually felt only on one side of the head, quite often behind the eye. As the headache develops there is a feeling of nausea and frequently actual vomiting. The attack may last for some hours or even days before passing off.

The migraine attack is due to a temporary constriction of some of the arteries of the brain which is soon followed by a dilatation of the same vessels. It seems that a number of factors combine to produce this effect, and that emotional stress is one of the most important of these factors. Of the patients with migraine treated by myself with relaxing methods to relieve tension approximately one third have practically ceased to have any attacks at all, one third have been markedly helped but still have some attacks, and one third were not helped at all. So it would seem well worthwhile for anyone who suffers with migraine to give the relaxing mental exercises a fair trial in order to reduce nervous tension as a means of relieving the attacks.

Painful Monthly Periods. A great number of women and girls suffer from this distressing condition, which is technically known as dysmenorrhea. There are different physical conditions which predispose toward this complaint, but in almost all cases there is an important emotional factor. If this can be remedied by reducing the patient's general level of anxiety so that she ceases to overreact to stress, the condition is usually cured or at least greatly relieved.

III

COMMON CAUSES OF ANXIETY

We have discussed some of the ways in which tension shows itself in the body and in the mind. We shall now consider some of the common causes.

SEXUAL CAUSES OF TENSION

At the present time there is a tendency to lay great emphasis on sex, and the tensions of both young and old are often ascribed to some disharmony in their sex life without due consideration of other factors. This line of approach is particularly common with the amateur psychologist. In evaluating the situation it is well for us to realize that sexual conflicts are in fact a very important cause of anxiety, but that conflicts in other areas are also important, and that anxiety often results from a summation of stresses arising from various problems.

There is another factor which makes it difficult to assess the significance of sexual troubles as a cause of anxiety. People have a tendency to give socially acceptable explanations for things. A man is working hard at his office; there are many difficult problems, and he has to work late at night. He will readily tell you this is the cause of his anxiety, and in a way it is true enough; but he does not readily discuss the tension he feels as a result of his being involved with his secretary. The patient often gives these false explanations quite knowingly for the simple reason that he is too ashamed to admit the real cause to the doctor. In other cases, the patient is too ashamed to admit the true cause even to himself. In these circumstances he believes that he is speaking the truth when he gives the socially acceptable reason as the cause of his trouble.

Masturbation as a Cause of Anxiety. Self-stimulation of the sexual parts is a common cause of anxiety in both men and women. The habit is almost universal in boys and young men before marriage, so much so that most authorities assume it to be a normal practice, one that causes harm only when done with excessive frequency—several times a day—or when it is associated with guilt from the warnings of overzealous parents. When there is a certain feeling of guilt, as there often is, the nervous tension may be extremely severe. The unfortunate youth is so ashamed that he tends to suffer his distress rather than seek help; and his fears may become so acute that he comes to think the habit will lead him to the insane asylum, or at least ruin any chance of happy marriage. Such people are greatly relieved by the simple and truthful explanation that a certain amount of self-stimulation seems to be a natural part of the ordinary process of growing up and leads to no harm of either body or mind.

However, in spite of the knowledge that a certain amount of self-stimulation is almost universal and quite harmless, it is my experience that some boys and young men still remain very disturbed by this practice.

This is an example of knowing a matter to be true with one's intellect and at the same time inwardly doubting it because the intellectual knowledge is not really integrated with the emotional life of the individual.

There are two categories of youths who consistently remain disturbed by their masturbation. There are those who are very rigid and fixed in their attitudes, who lack the normal flexibility of mind to change their view according to available evidence. They are often rather perfectionistic, and are technically known in psychiatry as obsessives. The other

group consists of young men who are taught by their church
that masturbation is sinful, and I do not believe that it is in
the province of the psychiatrist to challenge a patient's religious beliefs except under very exceptional circumstances.
Accordingly, these two groups—the very rigid and those
motivated by religion—are unable to adjust themselves to
occasional masturbation, and as a result they must stop it
altogether.

> A twenty-year-old student was in great distress of mind,
> worrying about his masturbation, which he seemed quite
> unable to control.
> Religious convictions were not involved here. The young
> man was extremely rigid and inflexible in his personality,
> so much so that in ordinary conversation he would talk
> obsessively about some particular topic. I showed him how
> to do the relaxing mental exercises. His nervous tension was
> greatly reduced. Now that he is calmer, he is able to use
> his will power with real determination, and has found that
> he has been able to abandon the habit which had caused
> him so much distress.

Adolescent Homosexual Experiences. At the present time
there is a fashion for frequent reference to the problem of
homosexuality in literature, in the theater, in films and TV.
As a result, the idea of homosexuality is brought to the minds
of many sensitive young people who would otherwise never
have thought of it. They begin to question themselves, and
come to worry about it, and they often think back to
some experience of their childhood or youth which involved
some degree of examination and experimentation with another of the same sex. Such experiences are common in the
youth of normal people, and in the vast majority of cases
do not lead to any difficulties in later life.

The opposite set of circumstances also occurs. There are
of course young men who do have homosexual traits in
their personality. But many of them are not aware of any

homosexual bias in themselves. These people are often chronically tense. Strangely enough their tension shows itself in different circumstances according to the degree to which their homosexual traits are repressed. They may become very tense in the company of girls of their own age, while with others the nervous tension is more marked with companions of the same sex because of the strange feeling of attraction which they do not understand or of which they may not be aware. However, the reader is warned that many sexually normal, but introvert, young people experience rather similar anxiety which is of no serious import at all.

Of course it is not uncommon for the young person of either sex to become aware that he or she is homosexually inclined, and then to marry in an attempt, as it were, to cure the homosexuality. In these circumstances a married life based on love and tenderness is virtually impossible, and both husband and wife soon develop the symptoms of nervous tension in greater or lesser degree.

This week I saw a tense young woman who was having difficulty in her marriage on account of her tension. She was working as a fully qualified professional psychologist. With a valiant effort to control her distress, she asked, "Am I a Lesbian? I have a girl friend whose company I enjoy very much."

She was greatly relieved when I explained that we all have quite normal homosexual traits hidden within us. It is only when these are grossly exaggerated that the individual is abnormal. If she had not been concerned with psychology, the thought of her being a Lesbian would probably have never occurred to her.

An intelligent young widow, the mother of three children, was desperately lonely for adult companionship. She came to enjoy a close friendship with a woman, who unbeknown to the patient was in fact a Lesbian. The widow enjoyed the friendship, and as a result her general health, mental

and physical, improved. Then suddenly the patient realized
that the other woman was a Lesbian. She was overwhelmed
with the most terrible panic and self-loathing in the belief
that she herself must be tainted.

Tranquilizers and logical explanation did nothing to relieve her turmoil; but as she learned to relax physically she
came to experience calm of her body in her mind, and
over a period of some weeks she regained her equilibrium.

A young university student arrived in great distress. Before coming to the point, he had to justify himself. "The
only way to have a full life is to have full experience of
life." He was rather a mixed-up youth, and had come to
associate with a group of pseudo-sophisticated students who
talked a lot about homosexuality. He had decided to put
this theory into practice. Quite deliberately he had sought
out a homosexual, had accompanied him to his flat, and had
had the experience he was seeking. Now he was in a pathetic
state of acute anxiety.

The theory of living the full life and of experiencing all
we can of life when we are young attracts many students
of both sexes. There are, however, two areas where experimentation frequently leads to disastrous results. These
are in homosexuality and in taking drugs.

Sexual Problems of the Shy Adolescent. Some people make
the various steps in sexual knowledge and experience from
childhood to maturity much more easily then do others. In
this respect the shy introvert typically has greater difficulties
than his more robust extrovert contemporaries. The introvert,
either boy or girl, is inclined to be timid and embarrassed
by matters of sex. As a result he withdraws from it. His
knowledge is incomplete, and his emotional and physical
contacts with the other sex are limited. He tends to fill in
the gaps in his knowledge by daydreaming. His uncertainties
and perplexities are increased, and the general level of his
anxiety remains high. Strange as it may seem, such a pattern established in adolescence may later persist through
marriage.

In an attempt to put an end to his complicated feeling in the matter, the shy introvert not infrequently decides to have a sexual experience. This usually lacks any spontaneous naturalness, and is often preceded by much thought and determination to bring himself to do it. The whole matter is out of character with his general personality, and instead of making things better the experience almost always has the reverse effect. The tension which accompanies it makes it physically difficult, and the sensitivity of the introvert adds guilt to his anxiety. Experience in psychotherapy with young people shows quite clearly that the inhibited introvert of either sex is greatly helped by talking over these matters with an experienced physician or psychiatrist.

I recently had come to me a young woman who was very shy—very nice, attractive in her quiet way, well-mannered, but painfully shy. Her brother is a doctor, and her sister happily married. Her parents, successful and easy in company, were socially ambitious for the girl. But she was held back; she just could not be natural with people. Then with tears and great distress she told me how a boy had touched her sexually, but really quite innocently. "I can never forgive myself." Then when she had pulled herself together, "How do you know where to draw the line?"

This is a problem that we all must face. She is twenty, but so timid and shy that she draws the line too high. And in her present state this must necessarily be so. We must not forget that different people need different solutions to similar problems according to their individual personality.

Sexual Experience Before Marriage. It takes a very mature person to be able to go against the established pattern of behavior of his group without experiencing inner tension, even when his own conscience is perfectly clear on the matter. The young person of either sex may become tense simply from the knowledge that his fellows are promiscuous. What passes for normal behavior in one group may cause offense in another, and what goes without thought in one man may offend the conscience of his brother. It is clear then, from the point of view of causing anxiety, there is no hard and fast rule. These difficulties of course are much greater when the two members of the couple come from different backgrounds and have different personal standards. The censure of the group, whether openly expressed or merely implied, causes tension; and this censure may arise from being too free, or from not being free enough, according to the prevailing morality of the particular group. With a certain amount of give and take the couple may be able to withstand these group pressures without tension. But the inner censor is more difficult to quiet. The idea of entering into sexual experience for the sake of one's partner, seems so plausible at the time, but it does little to dispel subsequent tension and anxiety if it conflicts with the basic personality of the individual.

It is well to remember that the tension of those in this situation is often greatly increased by the glib but well-meaning advice of their fellows, "Go ahead and get it over, it will ease your tension just as it does mine," is almost invariably bad advice. This is so because "going ahead" conflicts with the basic ideas of the individual. If this were not true, he obviously would have gone ahead before on his own initiative.

Some degree of anxiety from this type of situation is almost universal among young people. A medical student was so torn between the drive of his sexual urge and the dictates of his own inner conscience that he was on the verge of a serious breakdown. The situation was aggravated by his knowledge that most of his friends—real friends whom he respected—were promiscuous.

I talk to you merely as a physician whose concern is anxiety and tension—there may be others who would speak to you from a different point of view. Remember that different people have to find different solutions to the same problem. This is necessarily so because individual person-

alities differ. No problems are the same for everyone, and
the real decision rests in each individual self. For many,
these events are merely a necessary and commonplace experience in the process of growing up. They become something that helps to mature the personality, and as such
may come to bring fullness to a future marriage. But with
others the regret of past experience hangs heavily on the
mind. If this be the case, remember we cannot undo the
past. Let us accept it. As men and women we have all
done wrong. But any experience, however bad it seems,
almost always contains some element of good. Let us use
this element to enrich our personality. Even an event which
seems all bad—and I think this must be a rarity—may help
us from the experience of coping with such a situation.

Fear of Pregnancy. This is one of the most common causes
of anxiety in women of childbearing age. The unmarried
woman who has let herself be led into a foolish sexual experience without proper contraceptive precautions inevita-
bly experiences severe tension. Her anxiety is often sufficient to inhibit her next menstrual period. She sees this as
proof that her worst fears are confirmed, and desperation
and self-loathing may easily drive her into precipitate action.

The married woman who fears pregnancy usually says
that she does so because it would be financially embar-
rassing or would interfere too much with her social life.
However, on close questioning it frequently turns out that
there is much more to it than this, and that the fear is
really based on a deep-seated fear of childbirth which developed when she was a girl as a result of foolish talk on
the part of her mother or elder sister. That this fear is
in fact neurotic is shown by the fact that these women are
in no way reassured by completely adequate contraceptive
measures, and their intimate life with their husband leaves
them cold and in constant tension.

Contraception and Anxiety. The ready availability of re-
liable oral contraception has undoubtedly been a significant
factor in relieving tens of thousands of women of tension
and anxiety. On the other hand the advent of the contraceptive pill has brought tension and guilt to many women
who might otherwise have been free of it.

If a woman believes that contraception is morally wrong,
or if she is forbidden by her church to use it, and if she
follows her conscience in these matters and does not use it,
she may still suffer considerable mental tension arising from
her knowledge that women all around her are using contraception. As a result, she is constantly under temptation
in a manner in which other women are not. This is shown
by the way in which many such women do in fact take the
pill for a while, then feel guilty about taking it and stop.
Then they take it again, and in the same way discontinue
it; and so it goes on.

The position of course is much more difficult when husband and wife see the problem of contraception from different points of view. In such cases the unfortunate woman
may have contraception forced upon her without consideration of her inner religious feelings at all.

It is not uncommon for couples who have religious doubts
about contraception to feel that sexual withdrawal is less
of a sin than chemical means of prevention. But this half
measure only leads to further anxiety. There is still the
tension from feelings of guilt, and added to this the woman
is tensed fearing that her husband will not withdraw in
time. In addition, the fact of withdrawing just at the moment when biological fulfillment demands deepest penetration produces tension in both man and wife. This of course
has been known for centuries and was considered by Freud
as an important cause of anxiety.

There is yet another important social side-effect of the
widespread use of the contraceptive pill. Girls who have
been sexually promiscuous in the past are now relieved of

much of their anxiety. However, the ready availability of the pill has undoubtedly led many girls into promiscuity who would have otherwise been continent. Many of these young women suffer nervous tension not from doubts about taking the pill itself, but from moral qualms about their new way of life.

Problems of the Oversexed and the Undersexed. It is unlikely that any two individuals will have exactly the same sexual appetite. In this respect the early steps of marriage are a period of adjustment for almost every couple. It is common for the man's desire to be rather greater than that of his wife. He adjusts to a little less and she to rather more. However, sometimes there is a gross difference in sexual appetite which may remain throughout marriage and serve to keep both partners in a state of tension. In the less common situation in which the wife has the greater sexual appetite, her repeated demands may be particularly destructive to her husband because they psychologically threaten his masculinity.

If the adjustment of the partners one to the other is incomplete, the actual sexual experience itself may become a potent cause of tension. Thus if the sexual response of the husband is too rapid, his wife is left unsatisfied. If this pattern is constantly repeated the wife is likely to show signs of nervous tension and may develop any of the symptoms produced by anxiety.

> Many introvert men are not as sexually active as their extrovert brothers. An attractive woman with four children was married to an introvert husband who was some years older than she was, and who no longer satisfied her feeling of sexual need. She was tense and irritable, and disturbed by sexual feelings. She had an affair with another man. This, through guilt and fear lest her husband should find out, only increased her anxiety, and she soon abandoned her lover.

She gradually learned to cope with her anxiety and the disturbing sexual feeling by practicing the relaxing mental exercises.

A young couple who had been married five or six years consulted their local doctor because they were not getting on together. He referred them to me. The wife was an attractive girl, who covered up her tension very well. However, she openly admitted her irritability with her husband and the children. The husband was a big extrovert athlete, very much in love with his wife, and very willing to help in any way he could.

The wife eventually disclosed that she had come to dread going to bed. Her husband desired sex relations almost every night. Whatever her state of mind, she always created the illusion for her husband's sake that her sexual desire was as strong as his. This she was able to do because of her control over her feelings. The situation had eventually become impossible and she had broken down with anxiety. All the time the husband was completely unaware of his wife's sacrifice, and he was simply astounded when it was explained to him. He promptly reacted by curtailing his sexual appetite and heaping gifts on his wife.

Problems of Emotional Remoteness and of Too Close Relationship. Because of their different personalities different individuals express their feelings of affection in varying degrees of emotional and physical closeness. The shy and inhibited introvert habitually defends himself by withdrawing from people. In the early stages of marriage he is simply unable to tolerate a very close relationship. If his partner is emotionally freer, and is not sensitive enough to perceive his need for emotional distance, she may produce extreme tension in the introvert by trying to come too close either emotionally or physically. On the other hand, if the introvert's partner allows their relationship to develop slowly and easily, he will mature and come to make freer patterns of response which at first would have been quite impossible.

Sexual Pleasure in Causing Pain. The sex act evokes a different mental attitude in the man to that in the woman. The man is active and in a way aggressive, while she is essentially passive and accepting. In men, being active and aggressive may become associated with sexual feelings; but in another way aggressive action is associated with fighting and inflicting pain. In this way sexual pleasure may become unconsciously associated with causing pain, a condition known as sadism. The man with mild sadistic tendencies is rough with his sexual partner, and likes to penetrate roughly and deeply as if to hurt her. Conversely the passive and receptive elements in the woman may be associated with the idea of being hurt. She comes to experience sexual pleasure in being caused pain in her sexual relations. This is known as masochism. If the husband has marked sadistic traits, and if the wife is lacking in the corresponding masochistic elements, there will be tension and anxiety. If on the other hand these attitudes are reversed in an unnatural way so that the woman has the sadistic tendencies, then the tension is likely to be so much the greater because it conflicts more acutely with the male personality.

AGGRESSION AS A CAUSE OF ANXIETY

We all have a certain amount of aggression within us. If we didn't, we would not succeed as a species or as individuals. Man's aggression has led him to master the other animal species, and has to a large extent enabled him to control his immediate environment. However, the way in which man has progressed toward civilization has of itself imposed great restriction on his native aggression. He no longer has the opportunity to vent open aggression on animals that threaten him, or on a neighboring tribe who would take his food or his woman, nor can he turn his aggression on weaker members of his own kin and take what they have for himself. In our present evolutionary state man is struggling to control the aggressive impulses that are still within him.

This struggle with our own aggression is one of the greatest causes of tension. In many ways it is even more difficult to cope with than sexual problems, because while we usually have some awareness of our sexual difficulties, the struggle to control our aggressions may make us tense without us having any knowledge as to the cause of the tension.

A man of middle age came to see me for a skin rash which he had had on and off in front of his elbows and behind his knees for almost twenty years. He had had a lot of illness as a child which had left him undersized and with a bent back.

From the beginning he took charge of the interview. He was aggressive in his attitude, and rather contemptuous in his references to all the past failures of medical treatment. He mentioned that his family called him aggressive. He said that he loses his temper and blows up with his children, and then feels sorry for it. He added that he often drank heavily from sheer impatience and boredom. His wife disclosed that he really terrorized people—not only herself and the children, but other members of the family, and his friends at his place of work. The condition of his skin would wax and wane according to his state of frustration.

His aggression resulted from an inferiority complex, a reaction to compensate for his small size and weakly appearance. The anxiety engendered by his efforts to control his aggression had caused the skin condition.

Because he was so tense and aggressive it took him some time to learn how to relax, but when he did, his skin cleared up. A report from his wife indicated that those around him had come to have a happier time.

The Manifestations of Aggression. A man is angered; he goes to strike another, but is withheld by his friends. In such a simple situation we can see how his aggression was mobilized, and how it found direct expression. But aggression is constantly manifesting itself in much more devious ways: the indifferent manner of the civil servant toward us; our own authoritative attitude to the shop assistant; or in higher places, the judge's deliverance of a more severe sentence than the case would seem to warrant. These facets of behavior are all manifestations of aggression; so also are our forthright attitudes toward both minority groups and the established order of the state. When we talk too loudly or talk too quickly on a subject that affects us, it is aggression which motivates us. In fact, our aggression is continually influencing our behavior in an emotional way in all the small things we do in our everyday life. If we look for it, we soon recognize it in our friends, and with a little introspection we are humiliated to find the same force within ourselves.

Aggression in Childhood and Adolescence. This aggressive element is very deep-rooted; its beginnings can be seen in early infancy. Baby is happy when mother's milk comes freely and easily, but if it does not come quickly enough or if it comes too quickly, he is frustrated, and in a moment we see anger in his face, and his aggression is vented in crying and generalized movements of his body.

Different children react differently to parental discipline. One child's aggression may be aroused by a degree of discipline that would be easily tolerated by another. Anything which serves to make the child different from his fellows may arouse his aggression. Forced attendance at Sunday school, for example, or the failure of the parents to interest themselves in the matter, may worry the child and make him tense. When basic cultural or religious factors work to separate the family from others in the district, the child often suffers a smoldering aggressive reaction and his childhood may be marred by chronic anxiety and tension.

The adolescent is striving for adult status. He wants to be a man, and he is angered if he is still treated as a boy. He resents the controls which his parents and society exert over him for his well-being. This arouses aggression. To prove that he is grown-up he becomes defiant, and by his behavior unconsciously sets about to show the world that no one can tell him what he must do. There may be impulsive and quite unpredictable displays of aggression which may take the form of unnecessary and inappropriate self-assertion. Such behavior may alternate between the good-humored and the vicious. The company of young men of his own age with impulsive aggression similar to his own provides an easy milieu for the dissipation of his aggression, and we have the genesis of the teen-age gang.

Sometimes the aggressive behavior of the adolescent is easily explained. Recently a long-haired youth of nineteen was brought to see me by his mother and father because he would not have his hair cut. When asked about it quietly, he said that he really did not care if his hair was short or long; but he was simply not going to be told when to have it cut by mother and father. He was merely expressing his right to make his own decisions. Like many youths, this lad was very tense because he felt constantly frustrated by his parents in his attempt to achieve adult status; his aggression was aroused and found expression in his behavior and his way of wearing his hair. Many such lads lose their tension and come to behave in a more socially acceptable fashion when they realize what has been driving them to behave in this way.

The Control of Aggression. Aggression may be dealt with in various ways. It may simply be dissipated. We see this in simple form when a child is thwarted by his parents. His aggression is aroused, but he cannot give it direct expression or he will be punished. He is not mature enough to sublimate it. His aggression is just dissipated in his behavior. He stamps about, handles his toys roughly and expresses an aggressive attitude to those about him. In a more sophisticated way in adult life we dissipate our aggression by playing games or by watching sports in which we identify ourselves with the players and experience their emotions.

Aggression can also be displaced, so that our aggressive impulses toward one person or situation are vented on some completely innocent party. The husband is frustrated at work by his boss. His aggression is aroused. He cannot give it direct expression, but on reaching home he blows up and vents it on his unsuspecting wife. Aggression can also be controlled by act of will. In fact, learning to control aggression is one of the most important experiences of childhood and adolescence. But this control, and the awareness of the necessity for it, creates a further stress, and the individual is tense and anxious as a result of it.

The person who is controlling a good deal of aggression is vulnerable to minor additional stresses. This is an important factor in the cause of bad temper. Father tolerates the bickering of the children for a long time, then he suddenly blows up and punishes them more severely than he intended.

An intelligent adult man with a good work record came to see me, saying that he was becoming increasingly on edge so that he was likely to blow up with his wife and family at the least provocation. He had not realized that anything was wrong with himself until a few days previously. He had burst into a temper with his wife, and in the heat of his rage had thrown to the ground the watch which she had given him for his birthday. He then jumped on it until it was broken to pieces. He was humiliated and alarmed that he could have done such a thing.

With further discussion it became clear that he had been becoming more and more tense as a result of increasing pressures at work.

He went about practicing the relaxing exercises with real determination. His wife was understanding, and her support did much to relieve his sense of humiliation. She wrote to me some weeks later, saying that he was still doing the same amount of work, but things had never been better.

Many of us, perhaps all of us, have particular topics on which we are especially vulnerable. In these areas we are easily hurt, and our aggression is likely to flare up.

A man in his middle fifties held a responsible executive position, which he filled with reasonable ease and without any sign of undue aggression. He had always been extremely attached to his mother, so much so that it had been a constant source of conflict between him and his wife. The mother had died about a year previously, but instead of being better as one might have expected, things between the husband and wife were so much the worse. The wife had innocently suggested that he put away some of his mother's personal belongings. He had flown into a blind rage and struck her.

He was encouraged to do the relaxing exercises, and at the same time to concentrate on calm and understanding thoughts about his mother and wife. When I last saw him he was still a little touchy about his mother, but much easier than previously.

Aggression need not be such a destructive force. The same impulse that drives us to feel like punching someone in the nose can be diverted, and used to drive us on in whatever enterprise our life situation places us. By this drive we achieve goals in commerce, industry, and science. In a more personal way we obtain the drive to seek things out and to understand, both the material aspects of life and the abstract, in art and beauty.

Anxiety is the price we pay when our victory over our aggression is incomplete. But the reader who is seeking relief from mental tension is reminded that the struggle for inner control is not won by a fixed-jaw-and-clenched-fists attempt to discipline oneself at all costs. In this way we may manage to hold our aggression in check, and to stop it from breaking forth, but the effort of holding it in creates tension to the limit of our control. So, we must aim to establish a pattern of life in which our overt aggression is not easily aroused. We can do this by understanding the factors involved, by using our native aggression in creative fashion and by practicing our relaxing mental exercises. These three approaches are not separate entities but are a unity in themselves. Understanding, creative use of aggression, and ease of mind are one. This integration is to be our aim.

ANXIETY AND INSECURITY

We are all basically insecure, and this is the root of much of our anxiety. Our bodies are frail; therefore we can never hope for real material security. At any moment, even in the most protected situations, we may be stricken down with illness or death. Aware of this, man has sought another form of security—security in the sight of God. Such security can transcend the insecurity of life and death. But man has learned to doubt, the security of religious belief has ebbed from him, and as a result his latent anxiety and tension is so much the worse.

Childhood Insecurity. In childhood we are insecure because of our relative weakness compared with those about us. This childhood feeling of insecurity may persist, and form a pattern of tension and anxious behavior in adult life. Whether this will happen or not depends very largely on the degree to which the child perceives his early environment as threatening.

An interesting point in this regard is that the child withstands the evil influence of a constantly hostile environment better than he does an inconsistent one, where those around him are changeable, sometimes harsh and sometimes loving. In these circumstances the child does not know what to expect, and as a result lives in a state of chronic anxiety.

At school the child may be subject to influences which further increase his insecurity. These influences may be extremely subtle and may escape the notice of both teachers and parents only to be disclosed years later in psycho-therapy.

The native aggressive impulses of children are only just beneath the surface. They are easily turned on some less fortunate member of the group. Minor degrees of bullying may take a form that is scarcely perceptible to adults, but at the same time, may produce chronic tension in the un-fortunate victim.

Insecurity at Work. Man has evolved to what he is today through hundreds of thousands of years of insecurity. In fact, it would seem that we function best when we feel that we are not completely secure.

At work there is always insecurity. We may lose our job, or if we are self-employed, our business may fail. If this in-security reaches a certain degree we become tense and anxious. The sensitive are among the first affected, and those who are less gifted, less competent, and less well trained soon feel the strain. The situation is always worse when ag-gression is aroused. Because of our insecurity, our aggression has to be controlled at work, and as a result is likely to be displaced onto our wife and children at home.

A conscientious worker in a large industrial concern had been promoted to works manager. He now found that he had lost the fellow-feeling and security of being one of the men, and in addition he had to face pressures from both top management and union leaders. He broke down with chronic tension, depression, and sleeplessness. Relaxation helped him, and he was able to carry on; but when last seen he was still unable to attain real ease of mind, as he had really been promoted into a job beyond his emotional capacity.

Insecurity at Home. We think of home as being a refuge, a haven from the storms of the outside world. But this is not always so. Tension in the home is such a familiar theme

COMMON CAUSES OF ANXIETY

that it needs little explanation here. Sexual difficulties and the displacement of the husband's aggression onto his wife are common enough. But often simple insecurity is an important factor in the wife's nervous tension. She is insecure because she does not know how her husband will react: He is a different man according to whether he has had a good day or a bad day at the office, or whether he has had a few drinks on the way home.

A woman is more dependent by nature than is a man. She is therefore more vulnerable to insecurity when she is uncertain whether or not she can depend on her husband. This may apply to matters that seem quite trivial such as support on social occasions or help in controlling the children; but because of the need for support, she feels insecure and tension results.

There is obvious insecurity when the marriage is about to break up. But there are many less clearly defined actions which produce the same unease. The subtle change of attitude, the defensive reply, the inconsequential greeting, the vague reasons for this or that, and above all a lessening of sexual demands even when she herself has no particular sexual desire; these may all combine to produce a state of subclinical insecurity in the wife. She becomes chronically tense and ill at ease, perhaps without knowing exactly why.

ANXIETY FROM PERSONALITY TRAITS

The Perfectionist and Anxiety. The perfectionist unconsciously tries to ward off his inner tension by having everything just right. If everything is in order there is nothing to worry about. His efforts to be perfectly neat, scrupulously conscientious, and meticulously clean soon bring worries of their own, and at the same time fail to ward off his inner anxieties. The result is that the perfectionist comes to live a rigid and rather constricted way of life with a constantly high level of mental tension.

These difficulties are so much the more accentuated if the perfectionist is married to, or works with, a person who is freer and less restricted than himself. Then he is constantly ill at ease, wanting to clean up after his less orderly companion so that he can once again establish the pattern of having everything just right.

A patient who sought relief from inner tension fit this picture of the perfectionist. He was a jeweler, a modest and rather humble man, and extremely conscientious and fussy about his job, so that the work he produced was of exceptionally high quality. He had three apprentices working under him. In actual fact they did good work, and no one had ever found fault with it. But he was always worrying, fearing that it might not be quite perfect and wanting to check over the work of the apprentices just as he did his own.

With the relaxing mental exercises he was able to reduce his tension, so that he could carry on in relative ease, although he still remained very conscientious and a perfectionistic workman.

Anxiety and the Need for Dependence. As children we are all dependent upon our parents for our physical survival. So a pattern of accepting dependence is ingrained into us at an early stage.

Although we grow up into relatively independent adults, a need for some degree of dependence persists with us all. This is more obvious in the character of a woman, and has the biological function of allowing her to accept dependence when it is necessary for her during her childbearing period. On the other hand, the idea of being dependent on others may conflict with the aggressive and self-assertive aspects of a man's personality. Such men want to be independent of their parents or their wife, but at the same time they feel the need for dependency. They are caught in the dilemma of unconsciously wanting dependence and at the same time not wanting it. As a result they feel a tension for which they can see no reason.

Another cause of tension concerns the need to have others dependent on us. It is not uncommon for an emotionally mature woman to marry a man less mature than herself. He comes to rely on her, and to be dependent upon her. She in turn enjoys giving this support from the fullness of her maturity. However, it often happens when the couple have their first baby, that the wife switches, and gives her dependence to her child. The husband becomes tense; he is not quite sure what has happened. Those around him may see that his anxiety is due to the loss of his wife's emotional support, while he himself unconsciously saves face by not recognizing this cause of his tension.

On the other hand, a man who is a little immature may have fought hard to become independent of his parents in spite of his deep-seated wish to remain dependent. He succeeds, and has the feeling of well-being because his independence satisfies his masculinity. However, if such a man marries a mature, motherly type of woman, as he is often unconsciously driven to do, he may become tense again, because she, without knowing it, tries to develop a dependent relationship with him, which he unconsciously wants but at the same time strives to avoid.

In considering these different types of dependent relationships, it is well to remember that the mature person of either sex has a capacity both to give dependence to others and to accept some degree of dependence for himself. The man who would stand alone sees himself as the true picture of strength and maturity; but in reality he is a person who is not sufficiently secure to allow himself normal human interdependent relationships with his fellows.

A fifty-nine-year-old man who came to see me had always been extremely introverted and afraid of making a fool of himself in public. He had married a woman eight years younger than himself. She was a complete extrovert, and he saw in her all that he wished for himself. He developed a dependent relationship, but was unable to come close to her emotionally and was physically a poor lover. He covered up his feelings of inferiority with a good deal of aggression toward her. His wife eventually took a lover. He was shattered by the sudden loss of dependence, and he completely went to pieces, breaking down with acute anxiety symptoms.

The only thing in the world he wanted was to get her back. He worked conscientiously at the relaxing exercises. When his wife saw him more relaxed and without his former aggression, she abandoned her lover; and the story ends happily with the pair lovingly reunited.

They jointly sent a Christmas card with the note, "Christmas for us started on . . ." and then gave the date of their reunion.

Anxiety and Intelligence. We all have varying degrees of intelligence. But the extent to which we can use our intelligence depends very much on another factor, the integration of our personality, the way in which the different aspects of our mind work as a unity.

Those of us of less intelligence and less well-integrated minds find many ordinary everyday tasks quite difficult, while other more gifted people do these things naturally and easily without giving the matter any particular thought. The less gifted among us are therefore under a constant stress which others are not. As a result they remain tense, and at the same time are usually unable to see the cause of their tension.

Of course, this situation is relative. A highly intelligent person who is doing a job requiring exceptionally high intelligence is relatively in the position of being a dullard, and he experiences the same tensions as a dull person does in a less exacting job. Similarly, the intellectually backward individual may learn to live a useful and happy life as long as he can work and live in an environment which is not too demanding for him.

A disparity of intelligence between husband and wife may be a constant source of tension, especially when the wife is the more gifted one. Unless she is a very perceptive woman this disparity will lead her into a dominant role in the household which is likely to clash with her husband's masculinity and so produce further tension.

Anxiety and Conscience. When we examine the matter closely, we can see that most of the common causes of anxiety concern our conscience either directly or indirectly. This is clear enough in matters of sex and aggression, and it is only a little less obvious in the conflicts concerning dependence. However, very simple problems of conscience can produce tension in quite a surprising fashion.

It is common clinical experience to find that patients are tense on account of some problem of tax evasion. It is usually not so much a matter of frank dishonesty, but rather a problem of stretching the loopholes of the law to such an extent that inner conscience becomes uneasy.

Sensitive, introvert people who have something of the perfectionist in them are often tense because their life seems to lack fulfillment. They become overwhelmed by the material values that they find around them only to become aware that they themselves are lacking in any spiritual goal. They feel a sudden void; and they are anxious indeed.

It is not necessary to go to Africa as a missionary to fulfill these inner needs. But every sensitive individual, man or woman, if he is to remain free from inner tension, must make for himself some way of life which satisfies these vague needs of conscience and idealism.

IV

THE SELF-MANAGEMENT OF ANXIETY

GENERAL PRINCIPLES

We have seen that anxiety may arise from a great number of causes. When we come to examine them and understand them, we see further that many of the causes can in fact be remedied. This of course is the first step in the self-management of anxiety. Those causes that have a basis in external reality are the easiest to remedy. For instance, a perfectionist working in a job in which he is involved with dirt and untidiness will have much less tension if he changes to a more suitable occupation, or a couple may be able to free themselves of tension if they can make sensible mutual adjustments in their sex life together.

However, it is clear that many of the causes of anxiety are with us, and there is really nothing we can do to escape them. In these circumstances the mere fact of understanding the origin of our tension helps us to bear it. We must understand it in the full sense of the word. I do not mean that we have to know the technical psychological mechanisms involved. In fact this is really little help, as is proved by the generally high level of tension in psychology students. What is required is a kind of philosophical understanding—knowing the cause, together with a calm and easy acceptance of the situation.

Some tension, of course, may be due to an unknown cause, and this tension is much more difficult to tolerate because of our innate fear of the unknown. Our fear keeps prompting us to find the cause, and when we cannot do so, we begin to feel that we must be going out of our mind.

We see then that in some cases the cause of tension can be removed; in other cases, we cannot remedy the cause, but we can still reduce its effect by a proper understanding of the situation. In the vast majority of cases, however, we are faced with tension, the cause of which we can do very little, if anything, to modify. It is to those suffering with this type of tension, which seems so hopeless to most people, that this book is primarily directed. The approach is through relaxing mental exercises.

Do Not Be Put Off by the Simplicity. I have found that one of the greatest difficulties in helping people by this approach has been getting them to accept its simplicity. People always want the newest form of medical treatment. The modern trend in medicine is continually toward greater and greater complexity—more complicated instruments, more complicated tests, more potent drugs. We have come to associate complexity of therapy as an advance over more simple treatment. You can see my difficulty. I am advocating a form of treatment that is simple in the extreme. But I will remind you that it is natural as well as simple, and that is why it is so successful.

A very aggressive young woman, a graduate in psychology, was openly contemptuous when I explained the way in which I proposed to help her. She gave me a superior smile, and said, "It will take more than that."

I had great difficulty in persuading her to lie down on the couch so that I could show her what I meant. With a shrug of the shoulders, she said, "Oh well, just to please you!" I then spent sufficient time with her to be sure that she would capture a real feeling of relaxation. She did. This was the turning point. She learned to practice the exercises herself and did very well.

A writer of international fame consulted me because he was tense, disgruntled with himself, and had lost his creative ability. After considerable discussion of his difficulties, it seemed clear that the real problem was his inability to work caused by slowly mounting tension over the years. I explained how I could help him to be less tense and more at ease. However, he prided himself on his worldliness and his sophistication and from the outset was skeptical of my approach because of its inherent simplicity. He did the exercises, but he did them reluctantly, with a smirk on his face, as it were. He benefited to some extent, but I am sure his improvement would have been much more complete had he accepted the truth that we can often be helped most by basic methods which are themselves simple.

Please do not be put off by the simplicity of the method.

Relaxation. There is a close relationship between physical bodily tension and the sensation of mental tension. When we are worried over something we feel tense in our body; when we relax our body very completely we soon begin to feel relaxed in our mind. It is a common experience among psychiatrists to find that the patient who is losing his mental tension as a result of psychotherapy is physically more relaxed in his body. A basic principle of the relaxing mental exercises is the use of physical relaxation as a key to mental relaxation. This takes place in two stages. First we must learn complete physical relaxation, and second we must learn how to use this physical relaxation to promote calm and ease of our mind. Our mind relaxes following the relaxation of our body, and this mental relaxation tends to persist after we have ceased to relax our body. As the process is repeated the persistence of the mental relaxation becomes progressively greater and more prolonged until the stage is reached when it stays with us in all the tasks of our everyday living.

There is another fundamental factor. There are different kinds of relaxation. The kind of relaxation which leads us to calm and ease of mind is quite different from the relaxation which occurs when we lie down comfortably and doze off, perhaps even going to sleep. The type of relaxation which we want is essentially mental relaxation. This is independent of physical comfort. In fact it is more difficult to attain real mental relaxation if we are physically too comfortable, because we then achieve our feeling of relaxation through the physical comfort of our body and not by activity of our mind.

The type of relaxation which is most effective is different from the relaxation which leads to sleep. Of course, sleep itself is effective in relieving nervous tension. This is the first line of treatment which every doctor knows. He gives the nervous patient a sedative so as to ensure a good night's rest. Sleep eases the tension; but it is not nearly as effective in doing so as the profound mental relaxation in which the mind is deeply calm and at ease, yet at the same time fully awake.

The Mental Exercises Are Effective Irrespective of the Cause of Anxiety. It is clear that this approach is not directly related to the actual cause of the tension. This is an important point. At present there is a popular vogue that the only really satisfactory way to treat nervous illness is to unearth the cause. A little thought shows us that this is simply not true. Many people recover from nervous illness when they are given appropriate drugs, and we must not forget that religious experience, meditation, and philosophical practices have brought peace of mind to many who were disturbed. Furthermore, every psychiatrist knows that many patients can be brought to a full knowledge of the previously unconscious conflicts which caused their condition, but their symptoms still remain. Our own brief review of the causes of anxiety has shown that tension often results from a multitude of minor personal stresses of which the patient may be quite aware.

Our present approach to the relief of anxiety and tension by relaxing mental exercises works by aiding the natural processes of the body. It is effective irrespective of the cause of the anxiety; and above all else it is essentially a natural process.

Conditioning. Many people are quite prepared to follow advice and try some particular procedure simply if they are told that it will improve their health. On the other hand, more inquiring people will try something only if they are first given some explanation as to how it works.

In these days most people are familiar with the idea of psychological conditioning. The relaxing mental exercises work by conditioning the individual to a state of calm and ease of mind. There is also another conditioning mechanism involved. If some part of the nervous system is activated to produce a certain response, the reverse response is automatically inhibited; this is known technically as the principle of reciprocal inhibition. For example, if we move to straighten our leg, the muscles that work to flex the leg are at once inhibited, so that they are loose, and thus allow the easy straightening of the leg. The same principle applies to mental states. If something makes us happy, our sadness is dispelled. And the relaxing mental exercises inhibit the feeling of anxiety by the same kind of reciprocal inhibition.

There is a further mechanism involved in the relaxing mental exercises. During our life we learn certain patterns of reaction. We learn to make certain responses to certain situations. Of course, most of these patterns of reaction are learned in childhood, but to a lesser extent we continue to learn new ones throughout our adult life. The relaxing mental exercises are in themselves an experience. They become the means of learning a new pattern of response—the response of calm and ease of mind. The experience in the form of the exercises is repeated so that the response becomes fixed, and the individual comes to be aware of a calm and ease in his life which was not there before.

The Idea of Regression. Over the ages the mind of man has evolved from relative simplicity to greater and greater complexity. In a similar way the mind of the infant and child works in a much simpler fashion than that of the mature adult. But we, mature adults of the twentieth century, do not keep our minds constantly working at the full capacity of their state of development.

We often let our minds slip back, as it were, and let them work at a simpler stage of development—at a more primitive level. This is regression. It happens quite normally in our moments of reverie and when we are in the transition between wakefulness and sleep. It also occurs as a result of fatigue or mental illness or drugs or even alcohol. Essential features of regression are that we are less alert and that the critical faculties of our mind are less active. Regression to this kind of more primitive functioning of the mind is an important part of our relaxing mental exercises.

Let us for a moment consider anxiety from the evolutionary point of view. We have already learned enough about it to realize that it is a very complex state. Fear, on the other hand, is a much simpler emotion. We can see animals expressing fear, but it is hard to imagine that animals experience anxiety as we know it. The emotion with its attendant apprehension is too complex for their state of development. In other words, anxiety is a relatively recently acquired function of the mind—something that our prehuman primitive ancestors did not experience. In regression the mind goes back to a simple, primitive way of functioning in which there is an absence of anxiety. This is seen in our everyday experience. In moments of reverie and complete mental relaxation our mind fills with calm, and there is an absence of any feeling of anxiety.

We have discussed the way in which we learn various patterns of response during our life. Now, if we want to learn a new and better response to a certain situation, it is necessary that we first unlearn the old pattern of response.

We cannot simply add some new response to the old pattern, or we should develop some quite incongruous reaction. We cannot learn a new habit without first dropping the old one. In other words, before learning a new pattern of response we must first regress, and go back in our mind to the state before the development of the bad pattern of response. In our relaxing mental exercises we do this. We regress to a state of mind free from anxiety, and we are then free to learn the new pattern of calm and ease of mind.

This is the basic reason why explanation and persuasion are generally quite ineffective in helping those with tension. These are logical measures and work at an intellectual level; and they do not allow for the regression which is so necessary. As a result the patient can see the logic of what is explained to him, and he would like to do what we try to persuade him; but he cannot. He just remains as tense and anxious as ever because the all-important regression has been omitted.

In other relaxing techniques which are successful and in which the idea of regression is not actually mentioned, we can safely assume that regression occurs spontaneously without the patient's knowledge.

Integration of Impulses Arriving at the Brain. I have already mentioned that the basic cause of anxiety is the arrival at the brain of more nervous impulses than can be properly sorted out by the brain. In other words, there is incomplete integration of the impulses. A good sleep helps the brain in reaching this integration. We go to bed tense with anxiety, and wake refreshed and with things clearer in our mind after a good night's rest. Sleep then is a help in the integration of the inflow of nervous impulses. But a regressed state of mind is very much more effective in this respect than is sleep. This is clearly shown by the fact that people with severe chronic anxiety may be given drugs to make them sleep well; but anxiety of any severity is not relieved by this means. However, these people usually lose their anxiety if they can be brought to a regressed state of mind, and if they practice this consistently, the condition is gradually alleviated. In other words, the regressed state of the relaxing exercises aids the integration of the impulses arriving at the brain, and so reduces the general level of anxiety.

SOME PRACTICAL CONSIDERATIONS

There are a number of practical points which I always explain very carefully to patients. In addition, to be quite sure that I get these ideas across, I repeat them in different words each time I see the patient. The reason is that these practical considerations are so simple that the patient is likely to think, "Oh yes," and ignore the matter as too obvious to be thought about seriously.

I have another way of impressing these very simple ideas on the patient. I like to see the patient together with the person who is closest to him. If the patient is a man, I see him and his wife together; if it is the wife, I see her with her husband; young people I see with their parents; and the elderly with one of their children. I then explain these very simple things to them together. Then when the patient experiences temporary difficulty, or discouragement, he will naturally talk about it to the other person, who in turn will remind him that this is just what I warned him to expect. In order to apply this principle to your own case, I would suggest that you show this book to your wife or husband, and explain what you are doing.

With the patients whom I see in my consulting rooms I carry this principle even further. The patient and the person with him are sitting down talking with me while I explain things to them. When they are both fully at ease, I ask the patient just to show me for a moment how he can relax. He does this quite readily, as it fits into the context of our conversation. So it comes about that I give him his first lesson in his relaxing exercises in the presence of the other person. This helps to overcome a difficulty that many people experience. They tend to be rather self-conscious about doing their exercises. They seem to want to creep away and do them without anyone else knowing what is going on. It becomes a secret; and what is worse, it can become a kind of guilty secret.

One woman told me that she could do the exercises very well, but it was difficult to find the time, as naturally she could only do them when there was no one else in the house! This, of course, is a completely wrong approach; and I have discouraged it by having the patient do the exercises with the wife or husband sitting naturally in the room with me.

If you are a quick reader, now is the time to slow down a little, and let these simple ideas really sink into your mind. It would be foolish to miss the chance of real help by being too quick. Skimming through this is not enough. It requires more than that. The ideas must be absorbed. When I have the patient with me I see to this by repeating the ideas in different words and on different occasions. In your case, read it, go with it, let it seep into you, and re-read it again. Then you will see it work.

Do Not Expect Too Much Too Quickly. It is probable that you have had your tension or anxiety symptoms for some time. Do not expect them to disappear overnight following your first trial of relaxing mental exercises. You probably think it strange that I should give such a warning. But it is necessary. Experience has shown that many people tend to give up very easily. When I have personally been showing patients how to do it, and if they falter and show signs of giving up without a fair trial, I have been able to encourage them to keep going; and the vast majority have been well rewarded for doing so. But with you it is different. I can only be with you in spirit. Do not expect too much too quickly. It does not come all at once, neither the relief of your symptoms nor even the mastering of the techniques of mental relaxation.

In this respect it is well to remember that very dramatic changes in one's mental state, either for the better or for the worse, are in themselves evidence of instability. Be content with a slow and steady improvement.

Be Prepared for Ups and Downs. The graph of improvement from nervous illness is not a straight line. It is a graph that leads steadily upward, but at the same time has many minor ups and downs. This is inevitable until the initial improvement becomes consolidated. A very common pattern is one of improvement for a week or so, and then a down—a minor relapse. When this happens it is very easy to think you are right back where you were. But of course you are not. These minor reverses are simply things that we must learn to take in our stride as best we can. We can reassure ourselves in the knowledge that they will become less severe and less frequent until they cease altogether. Of course, I can help patients whom I see personally through these bad patches. In your case, just remember that they are part of the general pattern of getting well, and you will be all right.

Do Not Be Impatient with Yourself When at First You Cannot Relax. This is important. The relaxing is not difficult, but if you could do it in two minutes there would be no need for me to write these detailed instructions. It takes a little time to learn it. And in the initial phase while you are mastering it, you must be patient with yourself—and with me too.

There is one thing that you must not do. Do not under any circumstances say to yourself, "I can't relax; it might suit other people; it is not for me." In my experience almost everybody who is tense or who has anxiety symptoms can in fact learn to do it, and will receive help as a result.

There is another phase also when people often get cross with themselves. We first get our body relaxed, and then we bring the feeling of our bodily relaxation into our mind. Some people find that they can achieve bodily relaxation very easily; but the relaxation of the mind does not seem to follow it. They tend to get cross with themselves, and are likely to give up. The point to remember is this: Almost everyone—and I say "almost" only because as a scientist I must allow such a possibility—almost everyone who can achieve good physical relaxation of the body can go on and achieve similar relaxation of the mind. It only requires a little patience and persistence.

Bring Yourself to Like Doing It. The attitude of mind in which you approach your relaxing mental exercises is quite important. It is not a chore that you have to do when you would really prefer to be doing something else. There is no strain about it. Instead there is a feeling of ease. It is something that you like doing. It is something natural, something refreshing, something good; and you look forward to doing it, just in the same way as you look forward to any other pleasant experience.

Mental Exercises Are Similar to Physical Exercises. We all accept quite readily the idea of doing physical exercises to promote our physical health. This is almost a part of the way of life for many of us. The present procedure is merely a matter of doing mental exercises to promote our mental health.

It is interesting to note that the idea of doing physical exercises has a much wider appeal. It is simple. We can see what we are doing in physical exercises. But there is really no essential difference in principle.

Some systems which aim for spiritual advancement and peace of mind combine the physical and mental exercises. This is so with Yoga practice. The difficulty here is twofold. The physical element, the postures and the breathing, is not very acceptable to the Western mind. And I believe that this is rightly so, as there is something quite unnatural about it. Then there is a second difficulty of combining the physical and mental in Yoga. The Westerner almost invariably comes to concentrate on the outward physical part, and the inward meditative aspects come to be completely ignored.

It is best for our purposes that we cultivate the attitude of mind that our relaxing mental exercises are a matter-of-fact affair, simple and straightforward; and that we do them in the same easy and uncomplicated fashion as ordinary physical exercises are done.

Keep the Feeling of Relaxation During Your Everyday Tasks. It is good to achieve mental relaxation and calm during the mental exercises. But we want more than this. We want the calm and ease of mind to carry through in all the aspects of our everyday life. So once we have mastered the relaxation of our body and the relaxation of our mind, the next step is to consciously sustain the feeling of mental relaxation. At first it is easiest to practice this when we are doing relatively simple things, such as walking slowly along the street. During the course of the day when we have to pause or wait for something, we can consciously practice our exercises by allowing ourselves to recapture the feeling of relaxation of our mind. Although we have to do this consciously at first, we soon find that it comes naturally of its own volition. Gradually this ease of mind begins to penetrate all through us, as it were, so that it is with us in all that we do.

THE POSTURE FOR THE EXERCISES

The actual posture of the body has quite an influence on the effect of mental exercises. This applies particularly to our degree of comfort, the symmetry of our bodily position, and the movement of our body.

Assume a Position That Is Not Too Comfortable. Most people believe that the more comfortable we are, the more effective will be our relaxation. This idea is quite wrong. If we lie down comfortably on our bed, relaxation comes relatively easily. But as I mentioned previously, this type of relaxation has little effect in relieving our inner tension. When we relax in this way our relaxation is largely brought about by the physical comfort and warmth of our surroundings. Our body and limbs are supported comfortably by the soft bed. Nervous impulses arising in the skin, muscles, and joints report this state of affairs to the brain. As a result we feel relaxed. But this is not what we want. We aim for mental relaxation which comes from the mind itself. In order to achieve this we must not be too comfortable; if we are, our brain is swamped by comforting messages from our body and limbs, and there is little need for the mind to assert itself in this direction. In fact the most effective relaxation for releasing our inner tension comes when we achieve relaxation while we are slightly uncomfortable physically. In these circumstances the relaxation comes from the mind itself, and it is effective in permanently relieving inner tension.

A doctor came as a patient to see me, saying in a rather aggressive fashion that he had heard all about my relaxing methods. He had tried them; and they were not any good. When I asked him, he told me that he practiced lying down comfortably on his bed. When I explained the necessity for a more uncomfortable position he tried again and immediately was more successful.

I first realized the very great importance of this a few years ago. At the time I was traveling in India seeing what I could learn from yogis. They of course all meditate in the familiar cross-legged, squatting position known as the lotus posture. In all the books that I have read about Eastern religion and mysticism it is stated that this cross-legged, squatting position is comfortable for Asiatics. This is obviously true, as in India one sees people all around sitting comfortably in this position. But it is comfortable for the Indian only as long as he sits loosely in this position.

Yogis whom I questioned closely about their posture for meditation all told me that it was uncomfortable. I then learned that the meditating yogi keeps pulling his feet more and more tightly under his buttocks, so that in fact he is always slightly uncomfortable. My own experience, and my experience with patients, has taught me that some minor physical discomfort is very important in attaining effective mental relaxation.

A shrewd man who had had little formal education was running a large and successful business enterprise. Over the past few years he had become increasingly tense, and was compensating with alcohol. One day I asked him what he liked doing best in the world. His reply was, "Drinking beer."

I taught him how to relax and he learned to maintain his relaxation in uncomfortable circumstances while I was there to supervise him. But at home he would practice only when lying on his bed. He just lacked the necessary self-discipline to do the exercise properly. He actually made a good recovery, but it necessitated more visits to me than he would have otherwise needed.

Use a Symmetrical Posture. When we go to sleep, we usually lie on our side or curl up comfortably. People often tell me that they have been practicing relaxation like this. These are good positions for sleep, but we are aiming for deep mental relaxation which is different from sleep. Whether we lie down, or sit, or squat, our mental relaxation is more effective if we retain a symmetrical posture with our arms and legs in similar positions on each side of our body.

The Lying Posture. This is the basic posture and the easiest position for our exercises. We simply lie on our back with our arms by our side. Young people do not need a pillow. Adults can use a low pillow, but the lower the better, as lying quite flat enhances the feeling of abandonment—the letting go—which is such an important part of mental relaxation.

At the start a couch is quite suitable; but as soon as a real feeling of relaxation is attained it is wise to transfer to the harder surface of the floor. This is not quite so comfortable, and the relaxation achieved comes more from the mind and less from the body.

Lying on the sand on the beach is good; and the absence of clothes aids the feeling of abandonment. However, when we combine our exercises with sun-bathing, we want to distinguish between the two things. The mental exercises require controlled activity of the mind, but in sun-bathing we just let ourselves doze off, relaxed and uncontrolled.

The Sitting Posture. This is generally best for asthmatics and for middle-aged subjects. At first it is wise to use an armchair so that your arms can rest comfortably on the sides of the chair. It is best to sit up in the chair rather straight without the body slumped, which could tend to make the position too comfortable. The head can rest on the back of the chair. The legs are bent at the knees, and women find it wise to remove their high-heeled shoes.

When a fair degree of relaxation can be attained in an armchair, try a straight-backed dining-room chair. The head is now unsupported, and the forearms rest comfortably on the thighs.

The Squatting Posture. In this position we sit on a cushion cross-legged on the floor. Our arms can hang loosely at our sides or rest in our groins. The whole of our head, neck, and back is unsupported.

Try to keep the back and the neck fairly straight so that the muscular effort to maintain the position is reduced to a minimum. The cross-legged position usually makes enough tension on the joints to induce mild discomfort. As a result of these factors, relaxation attained in this posture is usually very effective. The position is very satisfactory for youthful subjects, and those who suffer from asthma, as it makes for easier breathing than lying down.

Where and When to Do the Exercises. We should fit the exercises into our way of life in as natural a way as possible. At first we want to do them in circumstances in which we ourselves feel secure. Otherwise we cannot let ourselves go off guard. This is important in the initial stages; then as we become more secure we can do them almost anywhere. Most men do them for five minutes before leaving for work, and then for a longer period after their evening meal. The housewife finds it best after she has gotten her husband off to work and the children to school. There is no need to be by one's self while doing them, and many husbands and wives do them while the other is reading the paper or watching TV. Mothers can do the exercises while sitting in front of the TV while the children are absorbed in the program.

About ten minutes twice a day is all the time required for the exercises. This is very little indeed. Yet quite a few people with real tension and distress of mind have told me that they have been unable to find the time to do them. Strange as it may seem, these are usually people whose time is not in any great demand. They are both sick and lazy; and because of their failure to find time for a few minutes' practice each day their condition drags on. I explain this to them, and they set about their practice in a more determined fashion. Their tension is eased. They soon come to do things more easily and quickly, and much time is saved.

Two business executives who suffered from chronic anxiety have independently learned to do the exercises as they sit in the train on the way to the city. A number of executives merely tell their secretary that they are on no account to be interrupted for ten or fifteen minutes. A factory worker told me that he retired to the toilet for five minutes twice a day so as to do the exercises, and by this means was able to manage his anxiety symptoms.

A works foreman takes his car in the lunch hour, drives to a quiet street, and does his exercises sitting in the car. Many people become tense in the muscles of the back and neck when they are driving. Such people get help by practicing conscious muscular relaxation as they drive along. Of course, they must first learn to do this by practicing the exercises in the ordinary way.

Undoubtedly one of the best ways is to let the exercises become a routine habit so that we do them regularly without thinking about it. For instance, I have had a number of patients who have made the exercises part of the routine of the morning shower. We get out of bed, and we do a number of things quite automatically—use the toilet, clean our teeth, wash our face, have our shower, dry ourselves, and put on our clothes. These events follow each other in routine fashion. There is no mental decision as to whether we clean our teeth or not, it is something that just happens by act of habit. Now let us establish a new habit. We come out of the shower; we get dry; with the towel around us, we sit on the stool, on the side of the bath, or we squat on the floor —just for three minutes—and we feel the relaxation all through us. Letting it become part of our regular routine ensures that we do not forget, and there is no mental effort in bringing ourselves to do it. After the shower we are fresh, and in a good state of mind for the mental exercises. Remember that it is better to do our exercises when we are fresh and alert, rather than when we are tired and weary at the end of the day, even though physical relaxation might come more easily then.

In addition, it is usual for those of us who are tense to experience a good deal of variation in our tension. We have good days and bad days. When we feel easy in ourselves we are inclined to forget that we were ever tense. As a result, on our good days it is common to neglect doing our exercises. This is a mistake. If we practice our exercises when we feel good, we ward off the bad patches. They gradually become less frequent and less severe. On the other hand, when we are unusually tense or upset we can get help by our mental exercises, but it is much more difficult to do them, particularly in the initial stages when we have not yet fully mastered the technique.

This principle is demonstrated very clearly in cases of asthma. During an asthma attack, particularly a bad one, it is quite hard to do the exercises. I therefore tell asthmatic patients that I can help them best by seeing them when they are not actually in an attack. I can then teach them the exercises easily. They practice at home, and the experience of many has been that the attacks gradually cease.

Those who do physical exercises soon learn to combine them with the mental exercises. This can be done in two ways. We can set aside a few minutes each day before we start the physical exercises. Alternatively, and this is a very good way, we can combine the two. As we do the physical exercises, we relax our minds.

Some people like doing the exercises while sitting outside in the open air. The sun is on our face, wind blows the hair, distant sounds come to us; we let go, and all this aids the calm and the integration within us.

People have sometimes asked how long they should keep doing the exercises. I suppose the answer is, "As long as they are doing you good." Many people find that the immediate problem ceases in a few weeks and they discontinue the exercises. Nevertheless, I think the exercises remain with them unconsciously, and become part of the mental attitude of their daily life. Others whom I have spoken to have kept doing the exercises regularly for long periods, saying that they feel the exercises help them in a more general way than just the removal of anxiety symptoms—that in some strange way they add to the quality of their living. I am sure you can see by now that this is a very different approach to illness than swallowing pills. Other things are involved which are very deep in our nature. The quality of the relaxation and the mechanisms involved will depend on the unique personality of the particular individual. But don't just drop the exercises at the first sign that your symptoms are subsiding.

THINGS TO REMEMBER

Now you are familiar with the various postures to assume while doing the exercises and you have some ideas about where and when to do them. Before going on to describe how the exercises are done, I want to review a few of the points we have been discussing. These considerations are so crucial to the success of the exercises that I want you to consider them again very carefully.

Relaxing Mental Exercises Are Not Difficult. I am going to spend some time in describing the relaxing mental exercises. Do not be put off by this. The exercises are not difficult. In fact they are very simple, and it is their simplicity that necessitates this rather detailed description because it is easy to go wrong from sheer inattention.

Those who are unimaginative might find an initial difficulty in accepting the idea of doing mental exercises. It may seem rather strange to them. But we all accept the connection between physical exercises and physical health, so let us try to accept the idea of mental exercises for mental health. Actually the idea of mental exercises is not as foreign to us as we may at first think. At school each of us have done arithmetic and algebra. Doing sums is itself a mental exercise the purpose of which is to help develop the intellectual powers of our mind. Some people practice meditative and religious mental exercises to develop the spiritual aspects of the mind. Our relaxing mental exercises aim to develop yet another aspect of the mind—the emotional.

Those who are rather lacking in ordinary determination have sometimes complained of difficulty in actually doing the exercises. They are usually people who want a thing done for them rather than to do it themselves.

A very successful businessman well past middle age came to see me because he had developed a distressing compulsion about checking over people's names. He was normally a robust, good-natured, jovial man, but had recently become tense, anxious, and depressed.

He had worked hard, and had been successful. Over the last few years he had grown to overindulge himself. He ate too much and drank too much. He liked the theater and television and the company of his friends. In short he was living for pleasure, and had lost the self-discipline which had characterized his earlier life. This man would do the exercises very well in my consulting room when I was there to supervise him. But there was always some trivial reason why he had not practiced at home. He settled down very well finally, but only because I continually kept him up to the mark. As you read this, please remember that this type of supervision should not be necessary.

It is also true that the medical profession has rather foisted the "easy way out" onto people by its readiness to prescribe tranquilizing drugs, rather than help the patient to cope with his inner tensions and learn to be relaxed. The relaxing mental exercises are not difficult. They merely require the minimum amount of patience which any new skill demands. If when you first try them, you are tense, don't give up; instead bear in mind that obviously tense individuals usually get the greatest benefit in the shortest time.

Ideas Have a Different Significance When Our Mind Is Regressed. When ideas are presented to us they convey a meaning. But the same ideas may have a rather different meaning for us according to our state of mind at the time. In our normal mental state we are alert and critical, and ideas that are presented to us carry their logical meaning. However, when we are very relaxed, and our mind has regressed, the same ideas carry a simpler and more fundamental meaning. This is a rather hard distinction to understand until we have experienced it. And it is not a difficult thing to experience. When we are doing our mental exercises we allow various trains of thought to come to our mind while we are very relaxed and regressed. In these circumstances it comes about that we *experience* the ideas rather than *comprehend* them logically. Furthermore, we experience them in a strikingly simple fashion. This is something quite different from the way the idea affects us in our normal alert state; and it is this that allows the exercises to influence us so profoundly.

I will describe various trains of thought which can help us is this way. Remember that these are expressed in a way for our relaxed and regressed mind to use. To our alert mind some of these sequences of thought may seem childish, odd, and repetitive. This may tempt you to reject the procedure as silly. Do not do this. The ideas are not written for your alert mind to evaluate and criticize; they are written for your relaxed and regressed mind to experience. That which may seem childish in our alert state becomes filled with simple and powerful meaning when we are a little regressed.

Relaxing Mental Exercises Are a Natural Form of Treatment. During the process of evolution we have developed ways of coping with difficulties. If we feel ill we go to bed. We do this as if by instinct. The rest and warmth give our body the best chance of dealing with the trouble. If we are tense, we rest and relax and soon we begin to feel less tense. These very simple measures have evolved over countless generations. They are part of us. They are our biological heritage. And in general they are very effective. The difficulty is that with advancing civilization and sophistication we have to a large extent lost our natural heritage. We have forgotten how to relax. Watch a cat relax, or a dog, or better still a South Sea Islander, and then we realize just how much we have forgotten.

Aim for Relaxed Activity. Remember that being relaxed does not mean living like a vegetable. On the contrary, it means a greater capacity to work, to do things easily and quickly and with a minimum of effort. Relaxation is an important aspect in the training of middle-distance and long-distance athletes, both runners and swimmers. While all the power of the body is being used, there is a feeling of relaxation of both body and mind, of rhythm, of ease of movement.

At different times I have seen a number of business executives who have complained of tension and irritability. When I have advised relaxing treatment, these men have often said that they do not want to be relaxed, or they would lose their punch, which, they said, was the key to their success as business executives. I explained to each that if he were relaxed and easy in his mind he would be able to carry out his executive duties even more effectively because his ability to be decisive would no longer be impeded by his inner tension. These men who tried the exercises now run their business empires without their former tension and irritability, without their ulcers, and with a good deal more graciousness to those around them.

The housewife can do her chores and still have energy left for other things; the student absorbs his studies more easily; the man at work tolerates his daily frustrations without fatigue and irritability.

How to Do the Exercises

We sit in an armchair or we lie down on a couch flat on our back. Our eyes are comfortably closed. We think to ourselves:

> It is good to relax.
> Relaxing is natural.
> It is the natural way to calm and ease.

Achieving Relaxation of the Body. We bring our body into relaxation by allowing the tension to go from our muscles. When we are in normal health there is always a certain degree of muscle tension. This is necessary to prevent our limbs flopping about in uncontrolled fashion and straining the joints. But when we are tense and anxious, this normal tension of the muscles is increased. So we start the relaxation by allowing our muscles to let go. As we do this we keep ourselves aware of the relaxation. In fact this conscious awareness of the relaxed and easy feeling is a very important part of all our exercises.

It is best to start with the big muscles of the thighs and arms because it is easiest to feel the relaxation in them.

You can test this now, as you are sitting reading this book. Just let your hand rest on your thigh. Now go to straighten your leg, but do not move it. With your hand you will feel the muscles of your thigh contract. Then you allow the muscles to let go, and with your hand you feel them relax. Now do the same thing without your hand on

your thigh. You are still aware of the muscles first contracting and then letting go. Sometimes, just at first, it is hard
to capture this feeling of letting go. But if you do this two
or three times you will soon come to feel it.

We can now start on our exercises. We present these ideas
to our mind:

> We think of our legs, the muscles of our legs.—We
> allow them to let go.—We can feel them relax.—We
> really feel it.—The muscles of our legs let go.—They
> let go so that all we feel of our legs is the weight of
> them on the floor.—They are heavy and comfort-
> able—the natural weight of our legs.—We feel this
> easy comfortable relaxation come all through us.—
> We feel it in our body.—Our arms are heavy on the
> side of the chair.—They are so relaxed we just feel
> the weight of them.—The natural weight of them.—
> Natural.—It is all natural.—Natural to let ourselves
> relax, and our mind learns to be calm and at ease
> again.—We feel the relaxation more and more.—It
> grows on us.—Our arms are so relaxed they hardly
> seem to belong to us.—Our whole body is relaxed.
> —We feel ourselves sitting in the chair.—Sinking
> into the chair.—We feel it in the face.—The mus-
> cles of our face relax with it.—Our jaw is loose.—
> It is so relaxed, so loose that our lips part.—We
> feel it in the muscles around our eyes.—We
> feel the muscles of our face smooth out with the
> relaxation.—It is in our forehead.—At the sides of
> our forehead, we feel it there deeply.

These are ideas which we present to our mind. We do
not just say them over, or repeat the thoughts to ourselves.
It is much more than that. These ideas all concern feeling.
We have the idea in our mind, and at the same time we

bring ourselves to experience the appropriate feeling. This is something very different from reading a paragraph and understanding it. Our exercises do not involve the critical faculties of our intellect. In the exercises it is a matter of presenting the idea to the mind, of receiving it, and experiencing it. We in fact experience both the feeling and the act. Thus the muscles of our legs let go, and we feel them let go. But the relationship of the act and the feeling is more complicated than this. For instance, the opposite is also true. We feel relaxed, and we are relaxed. Here the sensation precedes the act. What we aim for is an integrated experience in feeling and doing. Expressed like this, it would seem to be something difficult, and hard to attain. But it is not. It is natural and easy. Feeling and doing in this context are essentially simple and primitive. It is intellectual criticism of ideas which is complicated, and this has no part at all in our exercises. We merely have the simple idea in our mind; then we experience the simple feeling and the simple act that goes with it. We have the idea of our muscles relaxing. Then we experience it—really experience it—without the intervention of critical thought.

We need to repeat this exercise a number of times, and the feeling of relaxation becomes more and more a reality. But in repeating it—remember—there is no hurry, no rush; the whole thing is leisurely, easy, natural.

The sequence of the parts of the exercise follow quite naturally, so that they are easy enough to remember: the relaxation of the legs, the body, the arms, the face and the different parts of the face.

Remember that it does not all come at once. If at first you can capture just some of the feelings, the others will soon follow. Try to experience the sensation of weight in the legs as the muscles relax and let go, so that the legs seem heavy on the floor. The feeling of the face smoothing out as the facial muscles relax is another part of the exercise which comes quite easily. This is felt in the relaxation of the muscles around the eyes, and is enhanced by the letting go of the muscles of the jaw and the parting of the lips.

Achieving Relaxation of the Mind. We have already discussed the very close relationship between the body and the mind, and we have seen that relaxation of the body itself produces some relaxation of the mind. But we can go further than that, and we continue our exercises in this fashion:

> Our whole body is relaxed.—We feel it all through us.—It is in our face.—Our face is utterly relaxed.— We feel it in our forehead, and in the sides of our forehead.—We feel it there deeply, deeply in the sides of our forehead.—Deeply, we feel it in our mind.

This sequence follows on easily enough. We feel the relaxation in the muscles of our face, and with this relaxation we feel our face smooth out in calm. There is a very intimate relationship between the state of our mind and the state of our face. If your mind is calm, so is your face. Conversely if we learn to make our face calm, we experience a feeling of increasing calm of our mind.

With our jaw loose the muscles that work the jaw are fully relaxed. The two temporal muscles extend up to the sides of the forehead. You can feel them by placing the fingertips at the side of the forehead and firmly clenching the jaw. You can feel the muscle contract and then let go as the jaw is relaxed. The feeling of relaxation here gives us the feeling of relaxation deeply within us—in the mind itself.

> The whole of our body is relaxed.—We feel the relaxation of all the muscles of our body.—They are

relaxed.—They are relaxed and calm.—We can feel
the calm.—We feel the relaxation and we feel the
calm.—The relaxation is all through us, and so is the
calm that goes with it.—The calm of it is part of
us.—It is all through us in our body and our mind.

Again, the sequence is logical and straightforward. We
feel the relaxation of our muscles. Our relaxed muscles are
calm. We can feel the sensation of calm in them, we feel
the calm of it all through us. We feel the calm of it in our
mind.

Remember that the feeling of relaxation of the mind may
at first be variable. It may come and go. There may be a
momentary experience of calm of the mind and then it is
gone. This is to be expected for the first few attempts.
Remember that people who can attain relaxation of the
body can all learn to attain relaxation of the mind. If you
are able to capture just a moment of calm, it will not be
long before you can achieve the full state.

Remember, too, that relaxation of the mind is greatly
enhanced by physical relaxation which is attained in relatively uncomfortable circumstances. So as we become more
adept at our physical relaxation we do it in increasingly uncomfortable positions.

Achieving Regression. When we have attained relaxation
of our mind, we have already started on the way to regression. In regression we allow our mind to function in a
a simpler, more primitive fashion. The main features of this
state of mind are that we are less alert and less critical.
Regression of this nature is necessary to allow us to abandon
our old faulty patterns of reaction, so that we can learn
again new and better ways of reacting.

Remember that this regression of which we speak is quite
a normal process. We all experience it in our moments of
quiet reverie. At these times we let our mind wander, and

are no longer concerned with our immediate surroundings. In other words we cease to be alert and critical, and our mind is working at a simpler and more primitive level of organization.

We continue our exercises, allowing ourselves to neglect what is going on around us. We let ourselves lose awareness of the things in the room where we are. We temporarily abandon our critical faculties. If a truck passes in the street, we hear the noise, we don't think of it as being a heavily laden truck going past in the street; it is just a noise. This is what I mean by allowing ourselves to be uncritical.

We can now proceed with our exercises.

> We feel the calm of it all through us.—We feel it in our body; we feel it in our mind.—The calm pervades us.—We let ourselves go.—We let go, and we drift.—We drift in the calm of it.—Just letting ourselves go, we drift more and more.

This exercise is easy enough. It is merely a combination of two things which we have already achieved. We learned the letting-go feeling from the letting go of our muscles in relaxation. We have also learned to experience the feeling of calm in our mind as a continuation of the feeling of calm in our body. All we do now is combine these two. We let ourselves go in the calm. We do this, and we feel ourselves drifting in the calm that is all about us.

Like most of the different parts of the exercises, the drifting sensation does not usually come all at once in its complete form. Rather, at first, there are moments of drifting. Then it stops, and we allow ourselves to let go again, and the drifting returns.

When we achieve this drifting sensation, we have in fact regressed; in this state of mind we are no longer fully alert and critical as we are in our normal waking state.

> We let ourselves go with it.—We let ourselves go more and more completely.—Each breath, we let ourselves go as we breathe out.—We let go our breath; we let go ourselves, more and still more completely.

This is the general outline of the procedure. Each individual will make modifications to suit the particular needs of his own personality, his particular symptoms and the particular circumstances in which he is situated. As I have already said, it is important to get into the routine of just presenting the various ideas to the mind. Do not think about the ideas in logical fashion, as this prevents regression.

Difficulties in Attaining Physical Relaxation. The difficulties in attaining relaxation of the body are not great. But I think it wise to mention various difficulties that different people have experienced. Then if you find that you have similar problems you will at least know that others have also experienced them, and have overcome them without too much trouble.

The most common difficulty in learning to relax is undoubtedly the simple reluctance of many people to try it. I have had so many people say to me, "I really did not think that this would be any good for me, but you talked me into trying it, and now I am already feeling much easier in myself."

Another difficulty, as I have pointed out, is the simplicity of the procedure. Some people find it hard to believe that anything so simple and so natural could help them when they have already tried dozens of tablets and injections without effect. Do not forget that you too, by the very culture that surrounds you, have been at least partially conditioned into this pattern of thinking.

Restlessness may be a difficulty. We sit down ready to

start, and we immediately find we want to move about. We fidget. We move a leg and then an arm. Then we are aware that our clothes are uncomfortable, and we move again. Restlessness like this is only an initial difficulty. If you have this trouble, make yourself as comfortable as you can. Use cushions; lie on a soft bed—anything that appeals to you as making you comfortable. Then do your relaxation; but do it only for a very short period—two or three minutes. After that have a rest and a stretch, and then do it again. Soon the phase of restlessness will pass, and then you can move into doing the exercises in more uncomfortable positions.

The feeling of physical discomfort in some part of our body may cause difficulty in relaxation. We become aware of our leg. It is uncomfortable. It is beginning to hurt, and we feel we want to move it. At this stage, instead of moving it, concentrate on relaxing more completely. In spite of the discomfort we bring ourselves to let go more completely. We do this. We let ourselves go through the discomfort, as it were. The discomfort passes, and we relax more easily.

Sometimes a trembling of the muscles makes relaxation difficult. This is only a worry at the very start, and it soon passes. It is most common in the eyelids and the muscles around the eyes. In fact, some trembling of the eyelids would seem to be the general rule in the initial phases, and is of no consequence at all.

Difficulties in Attaining Relaxation of the Mind. It is extraordinary how people tend to give up even before they have started. "Relaxing the body, yes, I can do that; but relaxing my mind, that is impossible; that is why I have come to you." I hear this almost daily. Yet experience has shown that anyone who can achieve physical relaxation can likewise attain the sensation of relaxation of his mind, if he will only try—and try in the right way.

A common difficulty is that our thoughts seem to become

too active. We keep thinking of the problems of the day. All the small inconsequential things of our business keep running through our mind. In an effort to stop it, we consciously turn our thoughts to our home. But the same thing happens again, and we become exasperated by the flow of unwanted thoughts. This particular difficulty is more common in people who have well-developed obsessive traits in their personality. The main problem is the rather vivid awareness of these thoughts, the way they intrude into our consciousness and the way they disturb us. We cope with this difficulty simply by giving our thoughts full rein, as it were, and letting them wander where they will without us worrying about them. We do this in a way similar to what happens in our moments of reverie. In it we are idle, and we daydream. Our thoughts wander far and wide; but it does not disturb us, and we still remain completely relaxed in our mind. This is the approach to the difficulty of active thoughts while we are first trying to relax. We just let the thoughts go. There is no tension. We let them go easily, just where they like, and it does not worry us.

There is another approach to this same problem which is also a help. As we do our exercises we have to maintain the physical relaxation of our body. We do this by thinking of different parts of our body in turn, and making sure that each is relaxed.

> I can feel my legs relaxed, both of them relaxed.
> —My body, it is relaxed, and I just feel the weight
> of it.—My arms relaxed, my face smooth, my jaw
> loose, the muscles around my eyes relaxed, my
> forehead relaxed deeply.

The sequence is then repeated easily and leisurely, starting with the legs again. By this simple means the mind is kept occupied so that other thoughts do not get the chance to intrude and worry us.

Difficulties in Attaining Regression. Do not be alarmed at the thought of regression. Remember that it is a completely normal phenomenon which all normal people experience in moments of reverie. In fact, it would seem that periods of reverie, like sleep, are necessary for the normal healthy functioning of our mind. In moments of reverie we are no longer concerned with our immediate surroundings, and our mind is left to wander from topic to topic. These moments are extremely relaxing, and the relaxation of the mind remains with us for some time after we have abandoned our reverie, and have returned to our normal way of alert thinking. It seems that in reverie, just as in sleep, there is an integration of nervous impulses so that we lose some of our tension and anxiety, and as a result feel calmer and more relaxed. In this respect it is interesting to note that the person who suffers from severe tension and anxiety no longer has this normal tendency to moments of reverie. He is alert and on the lookout all the time. He cannot relax and let himself go off guard into a state of reverie. As a result he is without this normal mechanism which helps to save us from anxiety, so his tension is still further increased. The exercises with their consciously induced regression help to make up for the loss of spontaneous reverie, and so work to relieve tension and anxiety.

The common difficulty in allowing ourselves to regress concerns the letting go which is such an important part of it. There is a biological reason for this. Over countless generations we have been conditioned to be on guard. Those that were not on guard fell by the wayside and did not survive. True, we have some reverie, but reverie is characteristically a momentary affair. Now, to regress we have to let go and let ourselves be off guard. But now we can do it because we are safe. We know that we are safe and that nothing will befall us.

We are really rather afraid to let go. This applies to all of us, but especially to those who are tense and anxious.

When we suffer from tension we are all the time holding ourselves in, as it were. We keep a hold on ourselves. We keep ourselves in check. We feel that if we did not do this our tension would somehow get out of control, and anything might happen. The difficulty is that the anxious person is continually holding himself in, while in the exercises he is asked to let himself go.

There are two things which help us to overcome this difficulty. The first is that we know that we are completely safe. This simple idea is of the utmost importance. You are safe. It is perfectly safe for you to let yourself relax and go off guard, so that your mind can wander where it will. It is safe because it is the normal thing that all healthy people do in reverie. We must feel safe and secure, because if we feel unsafe and insecure we are automatically on guard, which is the exact opposite of what we are aiming to achieve.

The other way that we get help in allowing ourselves to drift into regression is to become more and more familiar with the sensation of letting go.

> I feel the muscles of my legs let go.—The thighs and the calves, they really let go.—My arms let go so that they are just flopped on the sides of the chair.—And the muscles of my face, they let go.— My jaw has let go, I feel it loose.—And my face lets go so that I can feel it smooth out.—I let go my whole body.—I let myself go.—I just drift with it.

Some people experience difficulty in that they remain too alert to everything that is going on around them. Their eyes are closed, but they are still conscious of the furniture and the things around them. If someone in the next room moves, they think that is so-and-so getting ready to prepare the meal. This is not what we want. We aim to let ourselves be oblivious of our immediate surroundings, and if we hear a noise from the next room, it is just a noise, and it has no particular significance for us. We can help ourselves like this:

> I am just sitting here relaxing.—While I am doing it nothing else matters, nothing else matters.—I am just here, easy, comfortable, relaxed.—There is just me relaxing.—Me relaxing, that is all that there is.

Occasionally sleep may be a difficulty. Some people, as they start to relax, go straight to sleep. This is to be avoided. Sleep is some help in relieving tension, but it is very, very much less help than this relaxed state of mind. If you have a tendency to fall asleep when you start your exercises, use a more uncomfortable posture, and concentrate on keeping awake. Then when you have finished the exercises, just let yourself drift off to sleep to have a rest.

More Advanced Exercises

Relaxing the Eyelids. For a number of reasons the eyelids are of particular importance. We have noted how over-alertness is one of the main signs of anxiety. A feature of being over-alert is keeping one's eyes open, so as to be on guard for any possible source of danger. The anxious patient characteristically has his eyes widely open, so that the edge of the upper lid does not cover the top of the colored part of the eye as it normally does. I have seen some patients with severe anxiety who have been so over-alert that they have virtually found it impossible to allow their eyes to close even for a moment.

It would seem that there is some such sequence of events as this. The brain is disturbed by receiving more nervous impulses than it can properly handle. As a result of this, a state of anxiety develops. The brain signals the eyes,

"Keep on the lookout. Keep wide open." From time to time
the nerves of the eyes report back, "Eyelids wide open."
It would seem then that the ideas of anxiety and wide
open eyelids become associated together in the brain. Now,
if we learn to allow our eyelids to remain comfortably in
a less fully open position, this will be reported to the
brain, and this state of affairs is associated with an absence
of anxiety. So instead of being over-alert, the mind becomes
calmer. This calmness of mind allows the better integration
of the nervous impluses, and anxiety is reduced. This, of
course, is only a more specialized example of the general
principle that relaxation of the body brings with it the sensation of relaxation of the mind.

While investigating these matters in the East a few years
ago I observed a number of very serene yogis whose eyelids remained in a nearly half-closed position, and whose
eyelids moved quite slowly, so that when they blinked their
eyelids moved slowly and leisurely. This extreme degree
of relaxation is, of course, dangerous in itself, as the protective value of the blink reflex is lost. Nevertheless, without
much effort we can encourage our eyelids to take up a more
relaxed position. If we practice this a little, we find that the
eyelids respond by developing this relaxed state quite
naturally and easily much sooner than we might expect.

When about to commence practicing our exercises we allow our eyelids to close. This is a natural, easy closure.
There is nothing forced about it. The edges of the lids are
just lightly touching each other. As we relax more completely, we notice that the eyelids part just a little so that
they are no longer touching each other, and we become
aware of a chink of light. This is the fully relaxed position
of the eyelids, and we should aim for this as we become
more expert in our exercises.

Some people do not close their eyes before they commence to relax. They are just left open. As relaxation becomes more complete the lids close very slowly over a period

of a few minutes. With this method, relaxation of the mind and a good degree of regression is obtained before the lids actually close.

Relaxation in Physical Discomfort. This is essential as we become more experienced in mental exercises. The aim is more complete relaxation of the mind. When we are in comfortable positions the relaxation of our mind comes largely from the feeling of bodily comfort. When we achieve this relaxation in situations of physical discomfort, the relaxation comes from the mind itself. This is what we aim to achieve.

We can practice in positions of varying discomfort according to our taste and the degree to which we have mastered the exercises. When we can do it well lying on the floor, we can try lying with a few pebbles under our back in the region of the shoulder blades. When we can do this, we are immediately aware of the much greater relaxation of our mind, and we soon notice that the relaxation remains with us for increasing periods in our everyday life.

In the sitting position we can put a small clip on the skin of our arm. We immediately relax deeply so as to avoid the feeling of discomfort. This soon passes off, and we come to feel a very complete relaxation of our mind. Young people can practice in the cross-legged, squatting position, and maintain a sufficient degree of discomfort by pulling their legs under their buttocks as the yogis do.

Combining the Exercises with Physical Activity. We naturally think of being quite still while we are relaxing. This is so for the early stages. However, we have now mastered the technique. We are familiar with the relaxed feeling of the mind, and we have learned to induce it quite easily and quickly while sitting down. We have now reached the stage when we can practice the exercises while we are actually doing things.

The first step in this direction is a very simple one. As we relax, we allow our eyes to open a little, and to close again very slowly. We do this in time with our breathing. As we breathe in our eyes open, then they close again as we breathe out. All the time we maintain the deep relaxation of our mind. At first we are content to have our eyes open just a little. As we become more experienced, they can open wider and wider.

The next stage is to do our exercises as we walk slowly down the street. We feel the relaxation of our mind. We are conscious of the ease and rhythm of our body as we move; and all the time we are aware of the relaxation of the muscles of our face and the calm of our mind.

In a similar way the housewife can practice while doing rhythmical domestic tasks such as polishing or using the vacuum cleaner on the floor. By this means the calm and ease of mind induced by the exercises is kept with us in all the tasks of our everyday life.

THE RELIEF OF SYMPTOMS

We have already discussed the mechanisms by which relaxation and regression of themselves work to reduce anxiety. Tension is eased, and so also are all the various symptoms which are the direct or indirect manifestations of anxiety. However, once we have mastered the relaxation of the body, the relaxation of the mind, and regression, we are in a position to use a more direct approach to the relief of symptoms and the promotion of better responses to life situations.

In its simplest form this consists of presenting to our mind very simple ideas for improvement while still in the relaxed and regressed state.

Regression and Sequences of Thought. We have discussed the idea of regression at some length as a process by which we drift back to a simple and more primitive way of mental functioning in which we cease to be alert and critical. In it we leave our mind to wander uncontrolled as in a state of reverie. Now that we have achieved this state of affairs we can go a step further. We can exert some control over our mind, but at the same time maintain our regression. This type of control must be very simple and primitive in itself, or it will bring us to be alert and critical, and our regression will immediately be lost.

The basis for the relief of our symptoms lies in the introduction of very simple trains of thought while we are still in our relaxed and regressed state of mind. It is emphasized that the trains of thought must be simple and direct or we will not be able to maintain our regression. The maintenance of the regression as we consider the train of thought is all-important. Without the regression the therapeutic train of thought has little or no effect at all.

What Makes the Mental Sequences Work. This is a matter of suggestion, and to understand how it works we must know something of the psychological process of suggestion.

Ideas can be accepted into the mind by two distinct mechanisms. We can scrutinize an idea that is offered to us, and examine it logically and critically. If we find it a good idea we accept it by this intellectual process of evaluation. On the other hand, many ideas are accepted into the mind quite uncritically and without any intellectual evaluation. We see this most commonly in children and in adults who are very relaxed, fatigued, or alcoholic. In this process the acceptance of the idea depends much more on our feeling toward the person who offers the idea than on the merits of the idea itself. The process by which ideas are accepted uncritically in this way is technically known as suggestion. It is important to remember that the uncritical acceptance of ideas in this fashion does not result from the evaluing mechanism working in less degree, but results from the activity of suggestion, which is quite a different mechanism of the mind. However, if the alert critical faculties of the intellect come into play, they always put a stop to suggestion, and the idea is subjected to the intellectual process of evaluation.

If we consider this matter from the biological point of view, we see that the critical method of accepting ideas is a recent evolutionary development, whereas the uncritical method based on our feeling for the other person is a biologically primitive process which has been practically superseded by this more recent development of our ability to evaluate things critically.

The important fact from our point of view is that this primitive process of suggestion functions very much more effectively when we have regressed a little toward a more primitive mode of mental functioning. This of course is exactly what we do in the regression of our mental exercises. So while we are regressed like this, we can use the process of suggestion to influence the working of our mind in a way that would be quite impossible if we were in our normal alert waking state.

In the matter of anxiety and general nervous tension our mind is quite impervious to the logical reasoned approach of the intellect, but on the other hand it is quite amenable to the process of suggestion when in this relaxed and regressed condition. In our exercises we ourselves present the ideas to our mind, so in this case the process is known as autosuggestion.

How to Use the Trains of Thought. In discussing the way to achieve bodily relaxation I described how the idea of relaxation is presented to the mind, and how we then experience the relaxation—both the feeling and the act. Once we can do it, this process is really quite effortless. The idea is in our mind, then we experience the effects of the idea. It just happens. We do not do anything to bring it about. In fact, once we make an effort to bring it about, the whole thing goes wrong, and we are immediately aware that we are not relaxed.

We use the trains of thought for the relief of symptoms in exactly the same way. The regression is the all-important factor. There is nothing new for us in this next step. We have already learned to present the idea of relaxation and then to experience relaxation. We can do this if we are tense, and our tension goes, because the positive feeling of relaxation will inhibit the negative feeling of tension by the process which we have already described as reciprocal inhibition.

The reader is reminded that the most effective way of doing the exercises with the trains of thought is to do them when we are relatively free of symptoms. To some extent our symptoms always vary. If we do the exercises in our good patches, it is much easier to do them, and we ward off the bad patches so that they are less frequent and less severe.

I have mentioned the method of letting ourselves go as we breathe out. We let go our breath, and we let go ourselves. With each breath we will drift a little deeper into regression. This approach can be used very successfully by some people to enhance the effect of their sequences of thought. We are very relaxed and comfortable. The ideas of the train of thought come to us slowly and leisurely. An idea comes each time we breathe out, and we dwell on it a little. With the next breath follows the next idea. And all the time we are so relaxed that we are hardly aware of the things around us.

The trains of thought, which I have set out in relation to various symptoms, are intended merely as a guide. They are only suggestions. Each individual will modify them according to his own inner needs. Only the principle is constant for us all. The details, the approach, and the attitude are varied to suit the unique individuality which makes each of us different from anyone else.

HELPFUL TRAINS OF THOUGHT

Now we can consider more specific measures for the relief of the mental symptoms of anxiety. We include in this all the various forms of mental disquiet which anxiety brings to us: tension, apprehension, restlessness, and all the strange variations of feeling which bring us to know that all is not well with us.

We use trains of thought which are most appropriate to our own particular circumstances. But we must always remember that the procedure is effective only when we are first thoroughly relaxed, and have let ourselves regress into this primitive type of uncritical thinking. Just going over these ideas casually as you read the book will not be sufficient, and will have no effect on your symptoms.

Concentrate on the Feeling of Calm. We are already familiar with this idea. If apprehension is a prominent symptom, as it often is, we can proceed like this:

> Relaxed.
> Whole of my body relaxed.
> Relaxed and calm.
> Calm all through me.
> Calm in my face.
> Calm in my mind.

Remember that it is not just a matter of repeating these ideas over to ourselves in our mind. We do it slowly, easily, comfortably, and really experience the feeling of each idea in turn.

Bodily Relaxation Leads to Mental Relaxation. This principle is a basic part of the relaxing mental exercises. When tension predominates we can use a train of thought like this:

> Relaxed.
> Whole body relaxed.
> Relaxation in my arm.
> Feel it in my mind.
> Feel my mind relaxed.

There are both physical and mental aspects to the feeling of tension. With physical relaxation the tension of our body subsides, and we experience the relaxation of our muscles. Then we feel in our mind the feeling of the relaxed muscles.

Start with your arm. Feel the relaxation in it; then feel this relaxation of your arm in your mind. Be sure that you are doing it properly. Feel in your mind the relaxation that is in your arm.

Relaxation of the Face Brings Relaxation of the Mind. We use to our advantage the very close relationship between the state of the muscles of our face and the state of our mind:

> Relaxed.
> Legs, arms, whole body relaxed.
> It is in my face.
> Jaw muscles loose.
> Muscles around the eyes are relaxed.
> Whole face smoothes out.
> Forehead relaxed—deeply.
> I feel it in my mind.

In all our exercises we make sure that we maintain relaxation of the face muscles because of their effect on our mental relaxation.

Relaxation Is the Natural Way to Peace of Mind. There
are many of us who feel we want to overcome our nervous
trouble through our own resources. We do not want to rely
on taking sedatives and tranquilizers over a long period. We
want a more natural approach to our problems:

> Relaxed.
> Natural to relax.
> It is the natural way.
> To rest, and relax, and be calm.
> Natural way to gather strength.
> Strength of body, and calm of mind.

Of course, this sequence of thought is absolutely true.
Relaxation is nature's way of coping with tension and anxiety. When we feel tense, something within us tells us to sit
down and relax. This is the simple biological remedy for a
very common condition. But the trouble is that when we go
to do it, we find it hard to achieve. Through our sophisticated cultural development we have lost the biologically
primitive art of simple relaxation. We need a little help to
relearn it again. This is the purpose of this book. It is natural
and simple; we just need this little help to learn again
what our distant forefathers could do so easily.

Emphasis on the Feeling That It Is Good. Ideas have a
rather different meaning for us—a different significance—
according to our state of mind when the ideas are presented
to us. At this moment, as you are reading this paragraph,
you are in a state of mind that is relatively alert and critical.
In this state of mind you read the heading "Emphasis on
the feeling that it is good" and quite likely you think
critically to yourself that it is a rather strange heading, a
strange idea. This is natural enough in your alert state of
mind. But remember that we are going to use this idea by
presenting it to ourselves when we are in an extremely re-

laxed, unalert, uncritical, and partially regressed state of mind. In this condition the idea, which now may seem rather odd and childish, takes on a new meaning of greater simplicity, and of deeper and more profound significance which quite eludes us in our normal state of critical alertness.

When we suffer from anxiety and chronic nervous tension, it is easy to feel that nothing seems good anymore. The luster goes from life. The brightness of the day has gone. Things that once brought us pleasure can no longer stir us. There may come a sensation of emptiness, the feeling that good has gone from us, and that we are indeed destitute.

We can let ourselves relax and help ourselves along these lines:

> Relaxed.
> Good to relax.
> Feel the relaxation all through me.
> Good to feel it like that.
> Really good.
> Wonderful feeling.

In our regressed state it is easy to experience the feeling of relaxation as good. When we have been tense and anxious for a long period, we come to forget that things can feel good. We learn to experience the feeling again in our relaxing exercises, and soon we find that our outlook is changing, and once more things in our ordinary life begin to feel good.

Experience the Feeling of Letting Go. Anxiety and nervous tension often make us restricted. We are tense, and we hold ourselves in check. We cannot let ourselves go. As a result of this we lose our normal freedom and ease of manner. It comes to affect us in all that we do, in our work, in our leisure, in our intimate life. We hold ourselves back, and try as we may, we cannot let ourselves go with the normal sense of freedom that we once enjoyed.

> Relaxed.
> I feel the relaxation.
> Feel the muscles let go.
> They let go all through me.
> It is in my mind.
> I let go.

The Feeling of Inner Strength. The effects of anxiety tend to destroy our morale. We may have had the condition a long time, and had treatment that has not helped us. We feel like giving in. But remember you can be promised at least some help from the practice of our relaxing mental exercises. So do not give up. When you are thoroughly relaxed, think along these lines:

> Relaxed.
> All my muscles relaxed.
> The calm of it all through me.
> I feel the calm and the ease.
> The calm that gives me strength.
> The inner strength.
> I feel the inner strength.

Remember the importance of the prior relaxation and regression. This is the key which opens the door of our mind to such ideas.

The Development of Self-Discipline. The way back to health from nervous illness always demands a fair degree of self-discipline. Some conditions require more, some less; and some of us find self-discipline easier than others. But we all need it for the struggle ahead, and we can help ourselves like this:

Relaxed.
Relaxed and calm.
The calm that gives us the strength.
The inner strength.
The strength to do what we have to do.

We can proceed further along these lines:

The inner strength.
It is calm strength.
Easy strength.
Easier and easier to be strong.

This of course is absolutely true. At first self-discipline is difficult, very difficult; but as we practice it more and more, it becomes easier and easier.

RELIEF OF PARTICULAR SYMPTOMS

Insomnia. Some degree of sleeplessness is a fairly constant feature of anxiety conditions. The main problem is that insomnia is such a disturbing symptom that we turn to sleeping tablets far too quickly. Most people can learn to use this relaxing technique to put themselves to sleep. I have recently been treating a doctor with chronic anxiety who had been taking sleeping capsules every night for twenty-five years. He learned the relaxing method of putting himself to sleep in three or four sessions, and since then has taken no sedative at night at all. But it does not come quite as easily as this to everyone. Give yourself a little time to get into the swing of it, and be patient when it does not all come at once.

When you have mastered the relaxing mental exercises, it is quite a simple matter to put yourself to sleep. You will have been practicing the exercises in relatively uncomfortable positions. Now do them when you go to bed, and with the added warmth and comfort they will seem very easy indeed. Just lie flat on your back and proceed with the exercises in the ordinary way:

> Relaxed.
> Legs are relaxed.
> Utterly relaxed.
> All I feel of them is their weight on the bed.
> Heavy relaxation.
> Heavy drowsy relaxation.
> It comes all through me.
> Heavy, drowsy, sleepy.
> My body is heavy with it.
> It is in my face.
> Eyelids are heavy with it.
> So drowsy, so sleepy.
> It is all through me.

When you really feel the heaviness, and the sleepiness, and weight in your eyelids, you just turn over onto your side into a sleeping position and you are asleep.

If you wake during the night, you just repeat the same procedure. It is important to do it systematically and in a relaxed fashion. Do not allow yourself to get restless or irritable with yourself. Do it systematically and you will soon be off to sleep again.

A feature of this approach is that it is effective not only with insomnia which is caused by anxiety, but with insomnia resulting from almost any cause. Those who are kept awake by pain find it very effective. Elderly persons can use the method with success provided their mind does not wander too much during the exercises.

Improvement in sleep is the general rule for anxious persons once they start to practice the exercises.

A rather outstanding example was a professional man who had been taking sleeping capsules every night for more than twenty years, since he was a student. He came seeking help for general anxiety, and his difficulty in sleeping was hardly mentioned, as he had assumed he would be taking sleeping capsules for the rest of his life. It was only afterward that he told me he had been so impressed with his calmer state of mind that he had experimented, and had gone to bed without his usual capsule, and was surprised to find that he could sleep quite well. He said that he felt that his sleep was lighter but at the same time more refreshing.

I can give a further example from my personal experience. The incident occurred just recently, after my first submission of this manuscript to the publishers. I developed an abscess on a tooth. My face was swollen right up to the eye. In spite of the pain I found I could put myself to sleep in two or three minutes by the relaxing exercises. However, in about half an hour, when I was deeply asleep and off guard, the pain woke me. But I was able to put myself asleep again quite quickly only to be awakened by the pain again in half an hour or so. This sequence was repeated several times during the night, so that I actually had a reasonable amount of sleep. Next morning I had the tooth extracted without anesthetic and without discomfort.

Phobias. Phobias arise through the individual's anxiety becoming attached to the phobic situation. This is rather similar to the way in which anxiety may become focused on some particular organ of the body and produce symptoms in it. Thus anxiety focused on the heart produces palpitation; on the stomach, dyspepsia; or on the lungs, asthma. In the case of the phobias we can often see quite clearly how the anxiety became associated with the particular situation. A child, punished by being locked in the broom closet, may develop a phobia of being confined in a small space. In other cases the anxiety becomes attached to the phobic situation through the mechanism of symbolism. Thus snakes and, to a lesser extent, mice, may represent important sexual symbols to some people, and a phobia of these animals may be a symbolic expression of anxiety which is in fact sexual in origin. However, bringing the patient to understand the cause of his phobia does not in itself relieve the patient's fear.

For instance, during the war in some bombers the rear gunners were locked into the tail gun turret by themselves. Many of these men subsequently developed a phobia of confined spaces. They would prefer to keep the door of the toilet slightly ajar. Of course, they knew the cause of their condition, but this did not stop the phobia.

We can use our relaxing mental exercises in three ways in the self-management of phobias. In the first place we practice our exercises when we are not in the phobic situation. Let us suppose that we have a phobia about going outside. We practice at home when there is no particular occasion for us to go outside. We do the exercises—very relaxed and letting ourselves regress—and as we do so we think:

> Relaxed.
> Whole body relaxed.
> Relaxed and calm and easy in myself.
> Easy in myself.
> Easy in myself wherever I go.

The exercise is repeated quietly and easily several times a day.

The second way of using the exercises is slightly different. As we relax we visualize ourselves at ease in the phobic situation. In our present example it means seeing ourselves in the street quite relaxed and comfortable. We do it very completely. As we relax we see ourselves; then as we relax more thoroughly, we see ourselves with greater and greater vividness. We are aware that we are calm and comfortable, and all the time that we visualize ourselves in this way, we are relaxed and at ease in ourselves.

Relaxed.
Utterly calm and easy.
See myself go out the door.
I am calm and easy.
Down the street.
I can see myself.
Calm and easy.
Nothing disturbs me.

In the third method we bring ourselves closer and closer to the center of the phobic situation. We go to the door. As we do so, we pause and capture again the relaxed feeling in our mind which we experience during the exercises. We go outside, relaxed and easy, and then we return. We repeatedly venture to the edge of the phobic situation. If we experience the slightest feeling of anxiety, we consciously recapture the relaxed feeling of the exercises. We do it easily. There is no panic. We do it little by little, more and more each day. The secret is that we do not allow anxiety to develop. Because of this, the conditioning process allows us to go further each day. Soon we are rewarded by finding that we are at ease in the phobic situation. But remember that this takes time, and requires a good deal of self-discipline.

On the one hand, we must make ourselves do it; on the other hand, we must not push ourselves so far that we become anxious.

As you read this, you probably think, "I have done all this before and it has not helped me. In the past I have tried like mad, and disciplined myself, but I am still the same." I must remind you again that the success of this approach depends entirely upon using the regression which comes with our relaxation. I believe that to overcome a phobia by self-discipline in cold blood is almost impossible. On the other hand, I do know for a fact that many people

have overcome phobias when they have used the regressed
state of mind to help them.

Mild phobias about moths are very common. They are
usually not very severe, and are often regarded rather in
the light of a slight idiosyncrasy and a matter for jest.
However, an eighteen-year-old girl was brought to me with
a severe moth phobia. She was in fact terrified of moths.
The phobia was so bad that it was ruining her life. She
was refusing to go out at night for fear there might be a
moth in one of the street lights or in any place of enter-
tainment.

While I was talking to her, she suddenly thought that I
might have a moth in the cigarette box on my desk. She
screamed in real terror, sprang from her chair, and rushed
to the far side of the room.

Because of her anxiety I had difficulty in showing her
how to relax properly. However, she eventually mastered it.
Then, when she was very relaxed I was able to show her a
moth without it disturbing her. Soon she was able to take
a moth in her hand. I don't think she ever really lost her
dislike of moths, but her phobia was relieved of all its
previous intensity and she was able to resume a normal
way of life.

A young professional man had a severe phobia about
leaving his home. As long as he was at home and his wife
was there with him, he was relatively free from anxiety.
But each morning when leaving home and going to work
he would be stricken with apprehension and panic. He
would sweat, and would be nearly overcome by the pounding of his heart and the feeling of his stomach turning over.
Once he reached his place of work, the acuteness of his
anxiety would pass until it was time to return home. He
had had a great deal of psychiatric treatment without help.

When I last saw him, he still had not gained complete
peace of mind, but he had learned to manage the worst of
his anxiety on his travels to and from his place of work.

A middle-aged housewife had become tense. As long as she remained at home she was relatively comfortable, and she had come to make excuses for not going out. The short trip to the shops to buy her household goods was becoming increasingly difficult. Sometimes she would stand petrified before bringing herself to enter a shop.

She learned to relax. Her general tension subsided, and she returned to doing her shopping without anxiety.

Speech Difficulty. Those of us who have difficulty with our speech can use the relaxing mental exercises to gain greater fluency. Those who stutter, and who are tense when speaking, can be helped because the practice of the exercises lowers the general level of anxiety. Tension is reduced and the words come more easily.

We can also incorporate our relaxing mental exercises into our speech therapy. We practice the exercises, and while still completely relaxed in both body and mind we count aloud—slowly, easily, clearly—and all the time we maintain the relaxation of body and mind. In the same way we can practice by reading and reciting.

Speaking on the telephone is often a major problem for those who stutter. This situation is very well suited for help from our mental exercises. As we take up the receiver our eyelids close, and we relax completely. We are leisurely, and we take our time before replying, and as we do so we feel the relaxation through the whole of us.

Difficulty in speaking in public is due to the mobilization of anxiety. The practice of relaxing mental exercises reduces our general level of anxiety, and also makes us less inclined to overreact to stressful situations. We thus come to have a little more in reserve, as it were, for the stress of making a speech. Sometimes a real phobia can develop in relation to making public speeches. In these circumstances we can get help by following the principles which I have set out for the self-management of phobias.

Some years ago a man from a country town came to see me on account of his speech difficulty. He was in his middle thirties. He had had two or three previous periods when his speech had been bad, but each time it had settled down in a matter of a few months. But this time it seemed to be getting worse. He was under increased stress at his work, which had made him tense, and his speech difficulty was associated with a jerky movement of his head. I had him relax several times in my consulting room and his trouble subsided. However, this was some years ago at a time when I had not realized the importance of the patient learning to do the relaxing himself.

He returned with a recurrence of his trouble a couple of years later. This time I showed him how to do it himself. His symptoms again subsided, and I have not seen him since. As he was very appreciative of the help I had given him, I think it fair to assume that he would have contacted me if he had had any further trouble.

If real stuttering is associated with anxiety and nervous tension it can be helped by this approach. On the other hand if you should be one of those who stutter in the absence of anxiety it is better to seek help through orthodox speech therapy.

A lad of eighteen had stuttered since he had first learned to talk. He was extremely tense and anxious, and when he would go to speak, his anxiety would seem to become quite uncontrolled. With the relaxing exercises over a period of some months he developed a rather careful, but almost normal pattern of speech.

On the other hand a man of twenty-six, with a terrible stutter, who had come some distance to see me, failed to obtain any material help at all. This man, unlike the previous patient, was really quite unconcerned about his stutter. He had no real anxiety. His purpose in coming to see me was that his firm had offered him a better job if he could get rid of his stutter.

Asthma. The history of medicine shows us very clearly that there is a recurring tendency for different forms of treatment to become fashionable and to be used overenthusiastically, often to the exclusion of simpler and more effective means of treatment. It would seem to me to be beyond doubt that this is the case with the present-day emphasis on allergy in the treatment of asthma. The basis for my conviction that other methods of treatment can relieve this affliction is simply that I have seen many people completely relieved of asthma following treatment by relaxation and regression. I have seen many others who, although not completely relieved, have vastly improved. Although allergic responses are an important factor in the cause of asthma, it would seem beyond all doubt that the treatment of the allergy by desensitization is not an essential part in the successful relief of the condition.

I really believe that if you suffer from asthma, you cannot afford not to take treatment by the relaxing mental exercises. But remember: Do not expect too much too quickly, and remember the course of improvement is at first subject to ups and downs. But in all probability you will soon find that the attacks become less severe and less frequent.

It is important to practice the relaxing mental exercises conscientiously in the periods between the attacks when your breathing is relatively free and easy. Do not wait until you get an attack to do the exercises. It is then often difficult to attain the relaxation and regression. The greatest benefit comes from doing the exercises when you are free of asthma. Possible future attacks are warded off and reduced in severity. If you should suffer an attack after starting the exercises, do not be discouraged by this. The relief of the asthma is usually a gradual process rather than an abrupt cessation of symptoms.

The relaxing mental exercises are effective in two ways. Asthma is usually associated with nervous tension. In fact, it is largely a psychosomatic expression of anxiety in a person who is predisposed to show symptoms in his chest on account of his inherent allergic condition. The exercises reduce the level of anxiety, and reduce the tendency to overreact to stress. We can also use the exercises in a more direct way. As we do them, we let the idea of ease come to our mind—ease of our body, ease of our breathing.

> Relaxed.
> All my muscles relaxed.
> Feel the relaxation and the ease.
> The ease of it all through me.
> The ease of it in my face, in my mind, in my breathing.
> Ease in my breathing.
> Breathing easily.

When starting the exercises, it is wise to continue with your usual medication. Only reduce your medication when you have got into the way of doing the exercises easily and effectively. Then reduce it slowly. This is best done in cooperation with your local doctor.

A fifteen-year-old schoolgirl had suffered from severe asthma for most of her life. Any effort seemed to produce an attack. She had to be driven to and from school although it was within easy walking distance of her home. Even the effort of carrying her schoolbag of books would be too much for her. After starting the relaxing exercises she had quite a severe attack of asthma, and I concluded that I had been little help to her. However, her mother called at my office some eighteen months later, just to let me know that the girl had continued to do the exercises, and was dramatically improved since her visits to me.

A twelve-year-old schoolboy was becoming dwarfed by the continual use of cortisone to control his asthma. He was very sensitive about this, and also about the obesity and changed expression of his face which the drug had induced. The exercises made it possible for him to discontinue the cortisone. He resumed growing, lost most of his fat and the moonlike expression of his face; and his occasional attacks are now quite easily controlled by orthodox medication.

Nervous Rashes. In general, nervous rashes are distinguished by the way in which the condition of the skin waxes and wanes with our emotional state. Sometimes we are rather blind to this, and only come to realize the relationship between the skin condition and our emotional state when it is pointed out to us by someone else. Then we wonder why we had not realized this before. A great number of chronic skin conditions are influenced in this way, particularly when we become frustrated by some stress and find ourselves in the position of being unable to do anything about it. This state of affairs is helped by the practice of our relaxing mental exercises, as this leads us to a calmer state of mind in which we are less inclined to feel frustrated by the various stresses of our life situation.

If we suffer a recurrence of our skin condition, we use our exercises to reduce our tension. We can also use the visualizing method:

> Relaxed.
> See my skin as it is, red and blotchy.
> Utterly relaxed.
> I see it clearly.
> It is fading.
> Utterly relaxed.
> Actually see it fading.
> See the skin normal again.
> Utterly relaxed, drifting in the relaxation.

Remember that to be effective the visualization needs to be combined with relaxation and regression.

Many doctors, aware of the emotional factor in the causation of chronic skin rashes, keep their patients on sedatives or tranquilizing drugs. When the exercises are practiced, it often happens that the rash subsides and the drugs can be withdrawn. In these cases, in order to avoid relapse, it is wise to continue with the exercises for some months after the rash has subsided, and until a more relaxed attitude of mind has been attained in which stress situations do not evoke in us the same degree of nervous frustration.

A rather pompous man had suffered from a generalized skin condition for some years. He felt that he was worthy of a much better job, but lacked the courage to make a change. It would take very little to make him feel slighted, and he was continually feeling humiliated and frustrated at work over matters of little consequence. The severity of his skin condition varied with these emotional upsets.

It did not take me long to find out his pattern of reaction, as at his first visit I inadvertently kept him waiting about five minutes. He was intensely angry about this, feeling that I was not treating him with due respect.

He learned to relax and his skin condition settled down. When he had become stabilized, I thought I would test him out. So I purposely kept him waiting for half an hour. He was quite relaxed about it, and when I reminded him of his anger on his first visit he only laughed.

A married man of forty-seven who held an executive position in an industrial concern was referred to me on account of recurring dermatitis of his hands. He had been tense all his life. He said, "I can't do anything to break the tension." However, he learned to relax very well and his dermatitis cleared.

Frigidity. Tension is the great enemy of free sexual response. Any woman who reduces her general level of anxiety finds that her sexual response is fuller, more spontaneous, and more satisfying. This is the experience of psychiatrists work-

ing with quite different methods of treatment. The relaxing
exercises reduce anxiety, and will work to increase a natural response, both physical and emotional.

There are, however, some particular exercises which will
help the frigid woman further. We have discussed the way
in which muscles are brought to relax, and at the same time
the relaxation is felt in the mind. Do the exercises lying on
the floor, and feel the relaxation in your thighs. When your
muscles are really relaxed your legs will roll outward from
the weight of your feet. Now feel the relaxation in your
mind.

> Relaxed.
> Legs rolled out.
> Thighs relaxed.
> Inside of them relaxed.
> Feel it in my mind.

You can go further than this by learning to feel the
relaxation of the parts concerned. Remember that this is
something quite natural. There is no reason to feel in any
way complicated about it. Most of us have been brought up,
either directly or indirectly, to avoid sensations in these
parts, to avoid feeling anything there at all. This of course
is probably a factor in your present difficulty. There are
two sets of muscles in which you can learn to experience the
"letting go" feeling. There are the muscles around the open-
ing of the vagina, and in the vagina itself. There are also
deeper muscles which stretch across from the bones in these
parts. Do not think that this is getting too complicated. Although you cannot see these muscles, you can quite easily
learn to feel them relax. It is the experience of this feeling
which helps you a great deal in the freedom of your response. Remember once again that this is a very natural way
of gaining help. We have been indirectly taught to deny

any feelings in this area. In a natural way we are just bringing our mind to relearn how to experience it.

It is easiest to feel the relaxation of these deeper muscles
if you do the exercises in a sitting position. The reason for
this is that the weight of the organs on the muscles pushes
them down when they relax, and then the sensation of their
contracting again is easily felt.

Do not think that I am involving you in something difficult. Actually it is remarkably simple. Just allow yourself
a little time and practice, and you will find that you can
relax and contract these muscles at will. At first the contraction will be easier to feel than the relaxation. Then when
you have the relaxation, feel it in your mind. More than
this, really experience it.

> Relaxed.
> Feel it there.
> Free.
> Free all through me.
> It's natural.
> It's good.

The freedom of the emotion follows the freedom of the
muscles. It may take just a little time, but if you stick to
it you will achieve the relaxation you want.

Premature Ejaculation. This is the condition in which the
man comes to a climax too soon. It is disturbing to the
husband and even more disturbing to his wife. It is a complaint which women often make about their husbands to a
psychiatrist, but rarely tell the husband himself for fear of
hurting his feelings. And this is very wise too, as many men
are extremely sensitive about such matters.

Premature ejaculation is a common symptom of anxiety.
In fact, when we are anxious all our responses come too
quickly—we rush at things, we move too quickly. If some-

one calls us, we turn immediately. There is no leisure about our reactions. It is the same in our sports. In tennis and golf we swing too quickly; when skiing we turn too quickly and the natural rhythm has gone from us. So it is in the sexual response. It is too quick. It is all over in a minute. There is no time for the easy flow of emotion; and both husband and wife are left unsatisfied. From talking with those who visit me, I believe that minor degrees of this condition must be very common.

The relaxing exercises reduce our anxiety. The special exercises concern the relaxing of the deep muscles of the parts which I have just described for the relief of frigidity. These muscles are basically similar in both men and women. In the woman they have to relax to allow free and easy penetration; and the feeling of this relaxation helps the proper emotional response. In the man, a similar relaxation of these muscles holds off the climax, and allows time for both his emotional fulfillment and the biologically slower response of his wife.

SUNDRY CONDITIONS

Smoking

A doctor came to me asking if I could help him stop smoking. I had steadfastly refused to become concerned with people's smoking habits. As a psychiatrist I wish to spend my time with those in more urgent need of help.

However, he seemed very sincere about it, so I agreed. I spent some time showing him how to relax. He was to come back again that afternoon without having smoked at all. He did this, and I was able to show him further relaxation. He was then to practice this at home in the evening and see me the following morning. Again he complied. He saw me the following day, and has not smoked since. This was four or five years ago.

Of course there is nothing very remarkable about this. But if you yourself wish to stop smoking, I would advise you to go about it this way. Set yourself a deadline, some day about two weeks hence, which is to be the day on which you will stop smoking. It is good to make it in the weekend or some day when you will have reasonable leisure. If you want to stop smoking, do it now. Now. Pause for a minute and fix the day. And in these two weeks learn to do the exercises properly—very completely. When you have mastered the physical and mental relaxation, and can let yourself regress a little, you can present ideas to your mind: smoking – silly habit – dirty habit – all that stuff in your lungs – unnatural – nasty – tastes nasty – smells nasty. Then on the morning of the allotted day throw away your cigarettes. And that is the end of it. There is no thought of giving in—no possibility of giving in. That first day you do the exercises quite a bit. You do them just to make yourself more comfortable, not because there is any doubt about the outcome.

Let us be quite clear about this. The basic difficulty in giving up smoking is that we feel we want a cigarette, and if we do not have one, we become tense. When we have mastered the exercises, we can control our tension, and it becomes relatively easy just not to have another cigarette.

Nail-Biting

A twenty-seven-year-old man sought help to stop biting his nails. He said he had had the habit ever since he could remember. He was extraordinarily tense, and he said he did most of his nail-biting when he was worried and on edge. He admitted that he was so tense that with little provocation he would flare up.

He did the exercises and when last seen about six weeks after his first visit claimed that he had mastered the habit, and as evidence showed me how his nails were beginning to grow normally.

Blushing

About two years ago an attractive nurse said she had been plagued with blushing for as long as she could remember. She often kept thinking about it and then she would blush. She blushed in the company of young men. She blushed in buses, and did not even like asking other nurses about patients on account of her blushing.

She learned the exercises, but I was not sure how much help she had gained until she came in a few weeks ago to ask advice about some other problem. When I asked her about the blushing she merely commented, "Oh, that's all gone," as if she had forgotten all about it.

It is interesting to note that some years previously I had seen a man with similar trouble about blushing. This was at the time before I had developed the idea of the patient doing the exercises himself. I treated this man with a number of sessions of hypnosis, and there was little improvement in his blushing.

Sterility

A twenty-six-year-old woman was frigid, but that was not what she came to consult me about. She had been married for three years to a man twelve years older than herself, and she desperately wanted a baby. She could not become pregnant. She had been very fully examined by gynecologists who could find no organic reason as to why she could not conceive, and she was told it must be because she was so tense.

She became pregnant about six weeks after starting the relaxing exercises, and subsequently gave birth to a baby girl.

This of course was a rather dramatic outcome. I expect the cynics would say that it was mere coincidence. But the patient and her husband believe beyond all doubt that learning to relax had allowed her to conceive. I think that they are probably right in this, as anxiety can cause contraction and blockage of the tubes down which the ovum has to pass.

Loss of Strength. When we are in normal physical health we are often unaware of the degree to which anxiety affects our bodily strength. This is so because in normal health we have an abundance of strength for our usual needs and our strength must be reduced quite a lot before we come to notice it.

This was very well shown in the case of a twenty-one-year-old student. The lad has a very severe congenital deformity of his heart, so that he can just manage to walk from one classroom to another without becoming breathless. At examination time he developed quite severe anxiety. Besides the usual feeling of tension and apprehension, his general bodily strength was affected so that he could no longer walk without becoming breathless, and in fact his strength was so reduced that he tended to become breathless in normal conversation. He learned to do the exercises. His anxiety was relieved, and he regained his former level of physical strength. His mother later wrote to me, thanking me again, and saying he had passed all his exams.

Writer's Cramp. Writer's cramp is a condition which is widely known to be particularly resistant to treatment.

A thirty-two-year-old single woman had a very good and highly paid job managing a large office. Over a period of two years she had developed writer's cramp. The condition had progressed to such an extent that writing was virtually impossible. She had been trying without much success to learn to write with her left hand. It was obvious that she was going to lose her job. She consulted her local doctor, who referred her to a leading neurologist. He wrote back to the local doctor, "As you know, this condition is somewhat a mystery and seldom responds to either medical or psychiatric treatment." However, he suggested that it might be worth her while seeing me.

I showed her how to relax, and while she was still relaxed, I gave her a large crayon, and asked her to make wavy lines. She did this, and was soon able to write with the crayon in a bold flowing hand. She practiced the relaxation, and in a few weeks was writing normally. I sent some specimens of her writing to the neurologist. He wrote back, "I do congratulate you, because writer's cramp in the past has been thought to be unmanageable."

But let us be clear about this. I did nothing to her beyond showing her how to relax in the way that is set out here.

Wryneck. Like writer's cramp, spasmodic torticollis or wryneck is a condition which is widely considered to be uninfluenced by any form of treatment. In fact, the most recently advocated treatment involves a destructive operation on the brain.

A seventeen-year-old schoolboy had this condition in quite advanced form so that his head was held twisted to one side with his chin over his shoulder. When for a moment he was able to bring his head to the front, there would be a sudden spasm of the muscles, and his head would be jerked to the side again.

I believe that this strange symptom had an unconscious symbolic meaning for the patient; and in fact it seemed that this lad was turning away from his father and the principles for which he stood.

I taught him to relax the rest of his body and to experience this relaxation in his mind. In doing this we had to ignore the spasm of the muscles in his neck. Then when he had mastered the exercises he was gradually able to bring his neck muscles to relax for a few moments, then for longer periods; until after several weeks of practice the condition completely cleared.

An interesting point was that the muscles on one side of his neck had grown to an unusual thickness as a result of the spasm. Some weeks after the spasm was relieved these returned to normal size.

His mother wrote, "I wish to take this opportunity of thanking you for the treatment you gave . . . earlier in the year. Without your help, I am quite sure he would not have recovered as he has done, and we are all very grateful to you. So far as . . . himself is concerned, he seems to be completely recovered, and his approach to life and its problems has, generally speaking, become much calmer and more reasonable than it was for some time past." At Christmas the boy sent a card, "It is wonderful to be able to do things normally again."

The mother spoke of the treatment I gave him. But remember that I merely showed him how to do it himself, just in the same way that I have set down here.

I have been a little doubtful of the wisdom of including these two cases—the writer's cramp and the wryneck—because it is so easy for people to say to themselves, "It is impossible that such a simple approach could cure such difficult conditions." Please do not be put off by the simplicity of this approach. Remember that the regression is an essential factor.

I have just recently seen a man with a wryneck condition, and I think I could have helped him. But he rejected the idea: "How could this help me, when all the other treatment has done me no good." The simplicity of the treatment is indeed its greatest difficulty.

Furthermore, please do not let the apparent diversity of all these conditions confuse you—nail-biting, blushing, writer's cramp, wryneck and even smoking. There is no diversity. They are all motivated by the one factor, anxiety. Our exercises reduce our anxiety and so allow the symptoms to subside.

Homosexuality

A man of twenty-two came to see me in great distress. He quite openly said that he was a homosexual. He had been caught by the police picking up another homosexual in a public bar. The police had been very considerate and had made no charge against him, but had advised him to seek the help of a psychiatrist, and to report back to them in a month.

In spite of his distress he kept saying that he was glad he had been caught. He described his furtive sexual life with casual men. He said he had been actively homosexual since aged twelve or thirteen. On one occasion four years ago, by great act of will he had had no homosexual experience for a month. On further questioning it became clear that he did not really enjoy these experiences. In a way he hated them. But he was so lonely, and so timid toward girls that this type of human contact was preferable to utter loneliness and isolation.

I explained to him that he had been driven to this form of sexual experience by his own introvert nature and not by true homosexuality. He learned to do the relaxing mental exercises. As his anxiety abated, he gradually became friendly with various girls. He found that he could like them and enjoy their company. It soon came about that he was talking of love, and he told me he was having normal sexual intercourse with the girl of his choice. With this there was a remarkable change in his personality.

This man had believed that he was destined to live a life in the shadows as a homosexual. Something happened to him beyond his wildest dreams. It is well to remember that there are many like him.

Irrational Behavior

At the age of fourteen a boy became increasingly fussy about things. He developed a number of fads, particularly about having proper exercise and special foods. If anything should happen to interfere with these matters he would fly into a terrible temper. He would become quite beside himself in rage. On many occasions he threw food on the floor, smashed crockery and did willful damage to furniture and household articles. He frequently hit his mother. However, both parents were extraordinarily tolerant of these outbursts which continued with increasing severity. In spite of this grossly disturbed behavior he did remarkably well at university entrance examinations, and obtained honors at the end of his first year. Nevertheless, the violence of his outbursts increased with greater damage to property and further assaults to his mother. So much so, that at the age of twenty he was certified to a mental asylum. After nine months in the asylum his parents were told by the authorities that nothing more could be done for him, and that he would probably spend the rest of his life in a mental asylum.

At this stage it was arranged that he should be transferred to a private hospital under my care. However, he had grown to rely on the security of the mental asylum, and he steadfastly refused to leave, and the authorities would not compel him to do so. This strange state of affairs continued for several weeks. Then he suddenly decided to go to the private hospital.

It was all very difficult. He was edgy and uncooperative, and for the most part refused any medication. His knowledge that at any time he could return to the mental asylum where he had felt secure did not help matters.

I eventually brought him to do the relaxing mental exercises. His tension was gradually reduced and he became more cooperative. In a couple of months he was well enough to leave the hospital and live in a flat of his own. A few months later he was able to resume at the university. The present indications are that he will finish his course with quite a brilliant scholastic record.

This has happened to a lad whose parents were told that he would have to remain in a mental asylum for the rest of his life. It became possible solely by the reduction of his general level of anxiety by the practice of the mental exercises.

FRINGE BENEFITS

A patient used this expression and it seems to suit the
situation very well. He had been married for three years;
he was not impotent, but was unable to come to a climax.
I had asked him not to have sex relations until he had
mastered the exercises. One day he came in and announced
that he was already getting "fringe benefits." He said that
he was much easier at his work, and added that his gait
seemed easier as he walked. He was in fact a big, clumsy
man with a rather awkward gait. His sexual difficulty cleared
up completely.

Fringe benefits are not occasional incidents but are really
the rule of the day. A patient who seeks help on account
of tension in the home, finds that he is easier at his work
and can do it more effectively. Many a wife has said that
her husband is easier to live with, although this was not the
cause of him coming to see me.

As our level of anxiety is reduced our sleep improves. This
is a very constant finding of those who do the exercises.

Many people have told me how their golf has improved.
When we are less tense we naturally swing more freely.
Patients who ski have told me that their turns have improved because they are less tense and can balance better
with more natural rhythm. I well remember the enthusiasm of a young stutterer about the improvement in his
baseball.

One of the areas where anxiety is first felt is in sexual
response. This is true for both men and women. Many patients have told me of improved sexual relationship when
they have actually come for treatment of some quite different
condition. Many of these people were in fact unaware that
there had been anything wrong in their sexual response
until they noticed this improvement. In more obvious cases,
men who had habitually come to a climax very quickly

found themselves no longer troubled with this difficulty. In the same way many women have reported more satisfactory sexual experience as a fringe benefit when having treatment for some other reason.

We should not be surprised at this. In fact it is exactly what we should expect. Anxiety always tends to inhibit the smooth working of our body, so as we reduce the level of our anxiety we should expect fringe benefits of this nature.

> I remember very clearly the case of a woman in her middle thirties who came to me to see if I could help her with her stutter. Her speech difficulty was associated with a good deal of tension and anxiety. She had had considerable psychotherapy and speech therapy without significant effect. In order to find out the background of her tension, I asked her about her personal life. She was very much in love with her husband and he with her, but her sex life was a complete failure, and she had come to look upon it as a kind of nightmare.
>
> I saw her six or eight times. Her speech returned to normal. On her final visit she explained that it was not only her speaking that had changed, but there had been a change all through her. When questioned further, she told me that she was now enjoying her intimate life with her husband in a way which she had not thought possible.

PART II

THE SELF-MANAGEMENT

OF PAIN

V

SOME NOTES ABOUT PAIN

We can learn to control pain in very much the same way as tension and anxiety, and this includes pain from organic as well as psychological causes. But before describing the self-management of painful conditions I shall discuss with you some particular aspects of pain. This will make it easier to understand exactly what we are doing when we start to work on the actual pain-relieving procedures.

THE BIOLOGICAL PURPOSE OF PAIN

Pain and Evil. We are likely to think of pain as something bad—something evil—that would not be present in a more perfect world. The ancients thought of pain as the tool of the devil, and a burden from which God would relieve them. All this, of course, is fanciful thinking.

Pain Is a Warning of Injury. Pain serves as much of a purpose as do our other sensations. Without hunger and thirst we would soon die of starvation; without a sex appetite our race would disintegrate; without feelings of hot and cold our bodies would be burnt and chilled. Similarly, pain is a warning that our body is suffering some harm. Without such a warning we would be unable to preserve ourselves from physical injury. So the sensation of pain is a helpful and necessary guide to us in our everyday living. If we remember this, and abandon any thoughts that pain is wrong or wicked or evil, it will help us in our exercises to control pain.

Excessive Pain. Of course, under some circumstances a warning may be too strong. As a psychiatrist I see examples of this almost every day. The child who is warned too much about the dangers of life may grow up to be a coward, and the warning has done as much harm as good. The little girl warned too strongly about boys may live out her life as a spinster, and what was intended well has done her harm. So it is with pain. Our body is not always able to regulate the strength of the warning according to the exact needs of the case. The pain may be too severe or last too long. Conversely, pain sometimes is not severe enough. This is so in the early stages of some forms of cancer. In these cases the disease may spread to other organs of the body before the pain is sufficiently severe to bring the patient to seek help.

Causes of Excessive Pain. Of course it is excessive pain which we desire to control, and which is the central subject of this study. A great number of different factors may combine to make pain excessive. Some of these are organic, depending upon the nerves concerned and their connections in the central nervous system; others are psychological and depend on our general mental health, as well as the particular significance which the pain has for us, both consciously and unconsciously. Constitutional factors also come into it. Some people are undoubtedly more sensitive to pain than others.

Some parts of our body are more copiously supplied with pain nerves than other parts. Any swelling due to inflammation is much more painful in a rigid tissue than in a soft tissue. This is so because pressure develops more easily in a rigid tissue. Thus an abscess at the apex of a tooth, or under the fingernail, is very painful, whereas a similar infection in the soft tissue under the skin causes relatively little pain.

If pain is coupled with distress, it quickly becomes excessive. It can be excessive, also, if it is associated with guilt, which often acts to prolong pain. The presence of a mild psychological depression makes the pain from some organic cause more severe, and tends to make the pain persist after the organic cause has ceased to operate. In fact, unrecognized depressive illness is one of the commonest causes of persistent pain for which no adequate organic cause can be found.

The Need for Severe and Prolonged Pain. We generally think of the sensation of pain as something we could well do without. When we are more thoughtful we can see the need for pain, but it still seems that pain as a warning sensation is much too severe and too prolonged. However, when we come to examine the situation more closely, we see that there is a reason for this. For instance, let us suppose that we burn our hand. The pain from the burn is sudden, intense, and severe. It overwhelms us and we immediately withdraw our hand. The pain is so intense that this reaction occurs automatically, quite beyond our control, and in the time of a split second. In this way the intensity of the pain causes the immediate withdrawal of our hand and so preserves it from further injury. We are not even given the chance to think about it. Thus, the severity of the pain is essential for its protective purpose. But the pain persists after we have withdrawn it from the flame, and is still so intense that we cannot even bear to touch the burnt area. This is again protective. By not touching it, we avoid bringing infection to the raw burn.

We sprain our ankle. The initial pain is so intense that we involuntarily fall to the ground, and our ankle is thus saved from further injury by immediately putting a stop to the stress which was tearing the ligaments. If we turn our foot in the direction of the twist there is an immediate recurrence of pain. So this movement is avoided and there is no further injury. This state of affairs persists for some days. The painful movement is avoided, and the torn ligaments are left undisturbed so that the process of repair can proceed in a way that would not be possible if the injured ankle was allowed pain-free movement.

TYPES OF PAIN

Organic and Functional Pain. Pain may arise from injury to our body cells. This is known as organic pain. More accurately it arises from the stimulation of nerve fibers as a result of injury to the body tissues. However, some organs of the body, such as the brain itself, are not supplied with pain nerves, and these organs can be cut or otherwise injured without causing any pain at all. In other instances, due to the complicated anatomical arrangement of the nervous system, the pain is not felt in the diseased part but is felt in some other area.

On the other hand, pain may arise in any part of the body as a result of the operation of psychological mechanisms within the mind, and in the complete absence of any physical disease or injury. This is known as functional pain.

It is important that we do not consider a person suffering from functional pain as *imagining* that he suffers pain. This is not so. He does suffer pain. Furthermore, functional pain may be very severe, and there is nothing in the quality of functional pain which automatically distinguishes it from organically determined pain. Although we can often tell one kind of pain from the other by the way in which it comes about or by the patient's reaction to it, we cannot always distinguish the two by the actual nature or severity of the pain.

Organic Pain with Functional Overlay. For descriptive purposes it is often convenient to consider pain as either organic or functional. But like many things in nature this pigeonholing of ideas is not completely valid. It is not quite as simple as that. Thus pain that is caused in the first place by some disease or injury soon produces a psychological reaction. It causes the patient to worry. He may worry a lot, or he may worry a little. The degree to which he worries will depend upon a great number of factors—the nature of his personality, and whether he somehow feels bad about his condition, or whether he blames himself for having caused it, or whether he feels that in being sick he has let down his family or others for whom he feels responsible. Psychological factors such as these influence the severity and duration of the pain. This is the psychological overlay that may accompany a pain which is classified as organic in origin in that it was primarily caused by stimulation of nerves by disease or injury. In fact, the psychological overlay may be the major factor in producing the pain in these cases, and it is not uncommon for the psychological overlay to maintain the pain long after any physical cause for the pain has ceased to operate.

This mechanism is often seen very clearly in cases of injury involving compensation. A man is injured at work. He knows that he is entitled to monetary compensation, but he does not know the exact figure until his claim is settled. The injury heals, but the pain persists. Sometimes the pain even gets worse. In spite of this he looks fit and well, but people near to him come to notice that his thoughts keep returning to this question of his claim for compensation. Doctors who examine him can find no cause for his pain, and they are inclined to regard him as malingering. Of course, everyone knows that cases of malingering do occur, but these represent only a small minority. The pain is determined unconsciously by the functional overlay without the patient having any real awareness as to what is happening. When no compensation is concerned patients recover from similar injuries without the same prolongation of the pain. Skeptics point to the fact that the pain clears up miraculously when the claim is settled, but this does not disprove the unconscious cause of the condition.

A man about forty-five years old was referred to me by his local doctor. The patient suffered from definite but mild rheumatoid arthritis. The local doctor was puzzled by the recent increase in the degree of pain suffered by the patient. It was little influenced by pain-killing drugs, and was on the point of ruining the patient's life.

The patient's wife was childless. Twenty years ago they had taken a baby girl to live with them. They had brought her up as their own, but the child's parents had never allowed them to adopt her. The girl was now to be married and the real father had come to take his place at the ceremony. The patient was tense, bitter, resentful, and full of unexpressed hostility. His tension had provided the functional overlay to the organic pain.

A childless woman of fifty had had minor surgery three years previously. She complained of pain in the scar. She had sought help from overseas specialists to no avail. She used the following words to describe her condition: "Feels like a knife or something sharp. Like a metal plate. Conscious of it all the time. It is an inhuman sort of pain. It aches at the base of the incision. Stiff and sore as if bruised."

She was a shallow society woman without any real sense of values, who for years had tried to escape life in an endless round of parties. Now she was older and no longer beautiful. She saw her friends with their children. The hurt of it all came to her, and she felt it in the scar of the operation.

I did not put these ideas to her. To do so would have been cruel, and would have made her worse by mobilizing her anxiety. It is usually unwise to tell people the cause of their trouble in so many words, much better to let it come indirectly; then they understand and know it to be true. This happened with this woman. She changed during the weeks she was doing the exercises, and it was clear that she achieved some inner acceptance of things in a way that is not uncommon when people come to do the exercises in meditative fashion. At the same time the pain subsided and she was able to resume a more active life.

Organic Pain from Psychological Causes. Sometimes when we are very tense in our mind we unconsciously hold our muscles very tensely. This may occur in driving our car. We may come to feel pain in our neck and shoulders. This is organic pain because it is due to the tense muscles stimulating the nerves; yet on the other hand the prime cause is psychological as the tense muscles are due to our tension of mind. The point that I wish to make is that organic and psychological factors are often closely interwoven in producing pain.

It is well known that fear, fright, or anxiety may cause diarrhea. Soldiers going into battle experience it, and to a lesser extent so do students facing an important examination. The diarrhea is of course caused by the contraction of the muscle of the bowels. Sometimes in these cases the contraction may be quite violent and uncoordinated. Pain results from the stimulation of the nerves of the bowels, but the contractions were the result of psychological causes. Such a condition is technically known as true psychosomatic pain.

A minor business executive in his fifties had been tense for some years. At periods of greater stress and greater tension he would be stricken with cramp-like pains in the stomach. The patient was well aware of the association of the pain with anxiety. This seemed to be a real psychosomatic pain in which anxiety caused intense contraction of the muscles of the stomach and so produced an organic type of pain.

He was a very enthusiastic patient, and in the course of four or five weeks lost all his pain and most of his tension.

This is intended as a practical little book aiming to help people to manage anxiety and pain. We must not get diverted into a complicated discussion of the relationship between body and mind. I think we have gone far enough to see that this is a very complex relationship, and as a result organic and psychological causes are continually interacting where pain is concerned.

I have mentioned that I have had teeth extracted without anesthetic. This would appear to be a matter of the control of purely organic pain. But it appears more simple than it is. The fact that I knew the dentist to be a kind, gentle, and competent person was undoubtedly a psychological help for me to feel no discomfort. So even in the simplest cases, both organic and psychological influences interact to determine the severity of pain.

Hysterical Pain. Hysteria is a condition in which some symptom develops which acts to solve some conflict for the patient. The conflict may be conscious or unconscious, and the symptoms may solve the conflict in some realistic way or may solve it only in some symbolic fashion, but in either case it usually does the patient harm in some other way. Very often the symptom takes the form of paralysis of a limb. For instance, a soldier may be approaching the enemy position. Naturally, he is afraid. He stumbles and falls; and suddenly finds that his leg is paralyzed. He is unable to go on. The hysterical symptom has served as a means of solving the conflict between his desire to do his duty and his desire to save himself. In a similar way pain may be a hysterical symptom.

The boy who has not done his homework suddenly develops a pain in the stomach when he is about to leave for school. It is real pain. He feels it and it hurts him. He cries with it. In fact this is a feature of hysterical pain; the sufferer has to let others know about it. These examples may seem very simple, but they are real; and we must remember that the soldier in fact cannot move his leg, and the child does in fact suffer pain. It is not altogether uncommon for adults to develop a severe headache when the time comes for some task which they do not relish. The circumstances may be such that the headache excuses them from the task; or on the other hand it may provide a ready excuse to themselves or to others for not doing it well.

Pain and Distress

The Pure Sensation of Pain. In ordinary circumstances pain hurts. Because it hurts we react to it. We therefore rarely experience pain in pure form.

I have warned you that some of these ideas are at first a little hard to accept. This idea is basic to our management of pain, so please go along with me.

You can actually prove this easily enough. Take a pin and stick it lightly into your forearm. It hurts, you screw up your face and perhaps say "Ow" under your breath. You would tell me that the painful stimulus hurts, and you react to it. This is not quite true. I do not think that there is a time sequence to these two events—the hurting and the reaction to it. I think they occur together, or the reacting may in fact precede the hurting. This is also easy to prove. Now decide to yourself that you will stick the pin in yourself again, but this time you will not in any way react to it. Make sure your face muscles are calm and easy. Now stick in the pin. Yes, you feel it. But this time there is no hurt. If we do not react to it, there is little or no hurt in the painful stimulus. At the same time we feel it. The sensation that we feel in these circumstances is some approach to pain in pure form.

It is important that we fully understand this, and know it to be true; so repeat the little experiment on yourself, and also do it to a friend.

We must conclude that pain is not an unbearable sensation, provided that we do not react to it. This is true of much more severe pain than a pinprick.

The Aggravation of Pain by Distress. The little boy is playing. He falls and skins his knees. He screams. In an instant his whole being is overwhelmed with pain. For him there is only pain, his whole body, his whole world. Mother seizes him and holds him to her, kissing him on the cheeks. In a moment his distress is calmed and the pain passes, the sobbing dies down and he returns to his world of reality, and inquires about the thing he was playing with. Mother has quieted his distress, and the pain of his skinned knees does not disturb him unduly. Remember that this comes about by her kissing his cheeks rather than attending to the injured knees.

You may say that this is all very well for a child, but I am an adult, and I do not react like this. Perhaps so. But we adults react to pain with distress, only we do so slightly differently. We stop ourselves screaming; but the pain is still there. In a way we scream inwardly, and while this is happening, like the child, we feel consumed by the pain.

We can get some insight into this by comparing different cultural reactions to pain. The Anglo-Saxon tradition is to present a stiff upper lip in the face of pain or disaster. On the other hand southern Europeans have an accepted tradition of giving vent to their feelings. Such a woman in childbirth may scream when she experiences pain, and give full vent to her distress; her Anglo-Saxon counterpart may lie there silent, but tense and blanched, and in obvious distress. Both are suffering severe pain because the element of distress has got out of hand whether it is openly expressed or not. Another woman may be led to relax in her mind. Then there is no distress. And because there is no distress there is little discomfort.

The Management of Pain by the Control of Distress. This, then, is a basic rule: Whatever happens in the way of pain we shall not allow ourselves to be overwhelmed by distress. This means that we shall not only prevent ourselves from venting distress, but more than this, we shall not allow ourselves to be inwardly overwhelmed.

At first this may seem a difficult task. But remember this. Distress is a purely psychological reaction, so it is possible to influence and control it by an act of mind, if we only set about it the right way.

The child is saved from his distress by the kisses of his mother. The woman in childbirth is led into a calm state of mind, and has her baby without discomfort. We understand the truth of these examples. But you quickly point out that in each case there is some other person who relieves the distress and so helps the one in pain. This is true. But let us think about it. The presence of the other person makes it easier, but he does not do anything that we cannot do ourselves. Really, what does he do? He communicates to us the message that we need not be overwhelmed by distress. The fact that he does this for us, helps us and makes it easier for us to master the situation. But it is still something that we can do ourselves. Many people do it simply through the natural intuitive processes of their mind; others can learn to do it by following these ideas, and letting themselves go along with them, and by experiencing the calm and ease of the mental exercises.

PAIN AND GUILT

Religious Aspects of Pain and Guilt. You may say to yourself, "I am not a religious person, so this section does not concern me." But the idea which I wish to discuss is religious in the widest sense, and applies to us all. It is like this. We have within us a number of very simple, primitive ideas which form a basis for our conduct of life as humans. Our sense of right and wrong is one such idea. The question of the origin of these ideas is beyond our present study, but they are ideas that are common to people of all religions including atheism. The particular idea that concerns us now is the feeling that sin is punished. I have referred to this as a feeling, because, with many of us, it is vague and ill-formulated, and is never really thought of in clearly logical terms. In fact, when we come to examine the idea logically, we are inclined to think that it is not sensible, and that we never really held such an idea. But it is there within us just the same. Our wickedness is punished. Wrongdoing brings pain. Then when we suffer pain, we think back, and ask ourselves, "What have I done wrong?" The idea is reflected in the expression which all doctors hear every day, "But what have I done to deserve this? Why should this happen to me?"

The Rationalization of Guilt from Pain. We suffer pain. We have the feeling deep down that wrongdoing brings pain. In silence we ask ourselves, "What is it that I have done?" In the long hours of the night when pain keeps us awake, we search the past. We have all done wrong. Our mind catches on to these things, and we become preoccupied with them. They are often sexual incidents of long ago. When day comes, and we have moments of freedom from pain, we can see these things for what they are—peccadilloes or incidents of life to which most of us are heir. But with persistent pain, the thought recurs. And sooner or later we become possessed of the vague feeling that the pain which we are suffering is somehow connected with our shortcomings of the past. It is seldom that these ideas are openly expressed.

If we are questioned on the subject, we immediately think about it, and as we do so the idea no longer seems sensible, and we deny feeling that way. But all the same the idea keeps recurring, vaguely but persistently. The evidence that this type of thinking commonly occurs in those with chronic pain comes from psychotherapy with such patients. These vague feelings, which are denied in answer to a direct question, are nevertheless divulged to the oblique but more penetrating probing of psychiatric treatment.

Pain and Punishment. The word "pain" comes from the Latin word *poena* which also means punishment. So there is nothing new in the association of these two ideas. The child is educated to a complicated system of values and behavior which allows him to take his place in society. This is achieved primarily by the process of reward and punishment. Love and physical rewards are given for being good; and hostility and physical punishment for being bad. This is the learning process in its simplest form, and as a means of leading the child to acceptable behavior it is very effective. However, the constant association of pain with punishment conditions us to lose sight of the biological purpose of pain as a simple and helpful warning against injury. The child is constantly reminded of this association so that it persists into adult life. If in fact corporal punishment is not inflicted, the threat of it is usually still there, and even if it is not actually threatened it is referred to obliquely, "If you had been properly punished when you were younger, this would not have happened." This is the child's ordinary experience, so the two ideas, pain and punishment, become fused together in his mind.

The Expiation of Guilt by Pain. When there is no clear cause for the condition, patients suffering from chronic pain are sometimes referred to a psychiatrist for his opinion.

When these patients really unburden themselves they often disclose that they are preoccupied in thinking about some wrong they have done in the past. Over the years they have thought about it a great deal, and in thinking about it in this way, the wrong becomes greatly magnified. They have never told anyone about it. "This is something that I always thought I would bring with me to the grave." And all the time there has been the thought, "Of course I shall be punished for it." In the first place the pain may have arisen from some quite trivial cause; but once the pain is there, it soon becomes fixed. Only half-consciously he thinks, "This is what I have been expecting; I knew it had to come; I am glad it has come at last and I shall get it over." In a sense he is glad of the pain. By suffering the pain he will ease his conscience of the thing that he has done, and his mind will be at rest again.

On the one hand a patient in this situation wants to get rid of the pain because it hurts him, but on the other hand he wants to keep it, as it expiates his feeling of guilt. The pain lingers on, unrelieved by the various medicines he is given. Expiation never seems complete, so it continues until brought to light and worked through in psychotherapy.

PAIN AND DEPRESSION

Pain is often associated with melancholia and depressive illness. There are two main types of psychological depression. In one type the depression results from a reaction to the loss of some loved one or to worry about some misfortune or wrongdoing. The other type of depression is not caused by any loss, misfortune, or wrongdoing, but comes on from some internal force acting upon us. But with severe depression there is a tendency to blame one's self. In this state of mind it is easy for psychological pain to develop. The patient feels depressed, he keeps thinking that he has done something wrong, and that he should be punished. He feels that pain is his just desert.

It is important to remember that if your pain is associated with mental depression that shows itself in a tendency to be tearful or just a difficulty in getting started at everyday tasks, then you should see your doctor. If the pain is in fact due to depression it is often effectively relieved by taking one of the new anti-depressant drugs.

We must be clear in our mind about the relationship of pain to depression. Sometimes depressive illness becomes the cause of chronic pain, at other times pain from some other cause brings about nervous depression.

Pain and Fear

Fear of Loss of Control. We live by a complicated code of social behavior. One aspect of it is that we should not give way to our feelings. With some people this is very important indeed. For instance, it is important for those in the armed services. The young soldier thinks, "If I am wounded, I hope I can take it like the others." In another setting we see the same thing with the young woman about to have her first baby. Thoughtless friends and relatives have led her to expect pain—very severe pain. She keeps thinking to herself, "I must not make a fuss; I must not give way; whatever happens I must not call out." In fact she fears that she will lose control. This fear of course increases her level of anxiety, increases her tension, and increases the pain.

Fear is also associated with pain in another and more significant way. We feel pain; and at the start we cope with it all right. But it goes on. We are not sure whether it is getting better or worse. We begin to think that it is more severe. Now fear begins to take over. What is going to happen to us? If it does not ease soon, something must happen.

There is a feeling of loss of control, and impending disaster. Fear runs wild, and the pain is increased a hundredfold.

Pain and Fear of Death. When pain lingers, another fear comes to us. Most of us fear death when faced directly with it, and lingering pain brings the fear of death even when the doctors assure us that there is nothing seriously wrong. Fear brings doubts: "Doctors make mistakes; and anyway they don't tell you the worst." If the pain is in the abdomen we are soon convinced that it is due to cancer; if it is in the chest we think of a coronary. Even when the pain is in some other part, if fear takes over, the same thoughts come to us. Strange as it may seem, in these circumstances the pain may spread so that we feel it in the heart, and fear leads us to think that the injury to our leg has brought on a heart attack.

The Destructive Effect of Pain. We can see, then, that instead of being a helpful warning against injury, pain that is too severe and too prolonged, when associated with distress and guilt and fear, soon becomes a destructive influence to both body and mind. It is only with the stoutest heart that morale does not weaken; and with failure of morale in any illness the healing process is correspondingly retarded. So anything that we can do in the way of learning the control of pain will not only boost our morale, but will also have an indirect effect on the physical healing of our body.

As an example of this process it is as well to recall that some years ago it was the custom to change the bandages on surgical wounds very frequently. This, particularly in the case of burns, would cause the patient great pain. The patient would wait in fear for the next change of dressings. Children would scream at the approach of the nurses. Even before the advent of the antibiotic drugs, the change to less frequent dressings improved both morale and healing.

Our Sensitivity to Pain

Pain in Man and Animals. We humans are inclined to regard
ourselves as sensitive in a way that animals are not because
our brain has developed above the level of that of animals.
We feel that we are sensitive, that we are highly strung.
This gives us the ability to appreciate the subtlety and
diversity of our sensations in a way which would not otherwise be possible. We feel that this sensitivity in itself makes
us more vulnerable to pain. I think that this is only partially
true. Many very sensitive people, by developing a quiet
philosophy and understanding, have a great capacity for
the self-management of pain; and on the other hand, many
very insensitive people allow distress and fear to overtake
them, and so withstand pain very badly.

My own experience with patients is that the more sensitive persons learn the technique of the self-management of
pain rather better than their less sensitive fellows. One reason for this is that some degree of sensitivity helps the
patient to let himself go along with me with these ideas.

Our Lost Ability to Cope with Pain. There is the evidence
of my own experience and my work with patients which
shows that we have within us the ability to control excessive
pain. But our everyday experience of life makes it equally
clear that under ordinary circumstances we are quite unable
to use this ability. It would seem that we, civilized people,
have somehow lost the knack of using it. On the other hand,
some primitive peoples still retain this ability to some extent,
and as a result cope with the pain of severe injury better
than the more civilized and sophisticated Western peoples.
This idea is quite important to our self-management of pain
because it makes us realize that we are not attempting something new and difficult, but instead are merely relearning
how to use an ability that we already have within us.

Our Lack of Experience of Pain. One reason for our relative inability to cope with excessive pain is simply our lack of experience in the matter. Life in Western communities is so organized now that we have very little firsthand experience of pain except an occasional visit to the dentist; and even he gives us an injection if he thinks it necessary or if we wish it. This is all a very wonderful advance in the history of man, but it has this unfortunate side-effect, that we are less able to cope with severe pain if it should befall us; and we turn more and more to the use of drugs for pain of less and less severity.

Preoccupation with Our Inner Feelings. In the history of man we have passed the stage of overcoming our natural environment. We no longer fear for food or shelter. We have paused, and have come to examine ourselves a little. We see evidence of our growing introspection in the great demand for psychology courses in our schools and universities, the introspective nature of modern literature and drama, and the subjective quality of modern abstract art. We are examining ourselves, and this is all to the good. But with it we are becoming preoccupied with our own minds and what is going on in them. Unless this increased introspection is accompanied by increased understanding, it leads to greater vulnerability to psychological stresses. Every psychiatrist must see this daily in his practice. Stresses which would otherwise go unheeded become magnified by our own introspection. A common clinical example is the way in which many women keep examining and pondering over their own sexual responsiveness. This almost invariably is the result of introspection after reading popular psychology, and it does little but increase the patient's anxiety and so further reduces her emotional response in the matter about which she has become so concerned.

The same may occur in relation to pain. The individual

who has become excessively introspective keeps examining his sensations. Minor painful stimuli which would ordinarily go unnoticed are brought into clear focus by his introspection. As a result there is a general lowering of the pain threshold, which is just the reverse of what we are aiming for in this study.

OUR REACTION TO PAIN

Different people react in different ways when they are confronted with pain. The way we react is important, as it has its effect on how we feel the pain, both in its severity and its duration. There are two very common types of reaction: the hostile and the depressive. Both have a bad effect and make the pain worse. These reactions come about unconsciously without our thinking about them, but a little understanding can do much to modify them, and thus help in the self-management of the pain.

The Hostile Reaction to Pain. "Why should this happen to me?" We hear these words often enough. It means the patient is reacting with hostility to the situation in which he finds himself. He feels that what he is suffering is an injustice. He is angry about it, and because there is no appropriate way for him to vent his anger he has to contain it. This results in an increase in his general level of anxiety. There is increased tension and increased perception of pain.

You have done nothing wrong. Do you think that some of these remarks could apply to yourself? If so, remember that we do not expect this sort of justice in other spheres of life. Perhaps we can expect something grander and deeper. Remember too, we strive for understanding; and when we can understand that some things transcend conventional logic, then we have come to understand something important indeed.

The Depressive Reaction to Pain. "I am like this because of what I have done." Unlike the hostile reaction the patient does not openly express this idea unless we first gain his confidence, and then bring him to talk quietly about his inner thoughts.

I have already explained this mechanism, and we have discussed the way in which pain becomes associated with punishment and then with guilt.

Have you had feelings like this, that somehow the pain is connected with the thing that happened long ago? If you have, face it openly. Remember that we have all done things that are wrong. And remember that psychological forces within us tend to bring these things to our mind, even when we suffer from pain that is due to simple and natural causes. So accept your pain for what it is—a warning of some injury to your body—a warning that has gone wrong and become too severe and prolonged.

The Philosophical Reaction to Pain. "It can't be helped. I shall get over it." This is the philosophical reaction. When we are free from pain we can see that this is the only sensible and mature way to respond. But when the time comes, and the pain is upon us, it is not quite so easy.

The philosophical reaction to pain is the attitude of mind that we must aim for. When we have this we have a firm base, as it were, from which to launch our self-management of pain.

How do we get it? By all the influences, great and small, that lead us to maturity. And of these influences there is none greater than understanding. And by understanding I mean something that is not necessarily of words, or of logic or of religion. It is that quality that the distressed patient refers to when he rises and says, "Thank you. I understand better now," when in fact I have said nothing to him about understanding. But he does understand better. It is shown in the way his distress has eased. This is what I mean by understanding.

THE PSYCHOLOGICAL APPROACH TO FUNCTIONAL PAIN

Understanding the Cause. One of the difficulties in the management of functional pain is that we find it very hard to accept the idea that the pain is in fact due to our nerves. We feel the pain; it hurts; it is a real pain. We are convinced in our mind that such real pain is not psychological in origin. We tell this to the doctor, but somehow he does not seem to understand. If he would only do some additional test we feel sure that it would show some organic cause for our trouble. We undoubtedly want to find an organic cause. Such is our scale of values that no one is very proud of himself when he has to explain to his friends that his pain is merely due to nerves. But there is more to it than this. The pain is so bad that we ourselves feel sure that it must be due to some physical condition of our body. This is particularly the case in psychosomatic abdominal pain. Our anxiety has affected the smooth working of our bowels. They contract in spasms, and often quite violently, and the part of the bowels in front of the contraction does not relax properly in the way that it should. The pain nerves in the bowels are stimulated and we experience real colic.

It is clear that the first stop in the self-management of such a condition is the acceptance of the idea that the pain is in fact the result of our anxiety. By acceptance of the idea I do not just mean verbal agreement with our doctor. It is very easy to do this, and at the same time to keep our own reservations on the matter. No. We must accept the truth openly and without reservation.

There is a further point that needs explanation. We are often inclined to think that our pain should be directly related to the cause of our anxiety. For instance, if our anxiety is caused by a sexual conflict, as it often is, then we might expect it to show itself in pain in the sexual parts rather than in pain in the stomach. But this is not so. There are usually two factors: one is the conflict or conflicts which produce our anxiety; and the other is usually some incidental matter, such as past trouble in some organ, so that our attention is focused there in a way that has the effect of localizing our psychological pain in this part of our body.

Resolving the Conflict. It makes it easier to resolve our conflicts if there is someone we can trust to whom we can unburden ourselves. This, of course, is the basis of psychotherapy. However, there are quite a number of people who are disturbed by functional pain which is due to anxiety from causes which are clearly within their consciousness. As I write, two patients come to my mind, one a man, the other a woman. In both the conflict concerned an extramarital love affair. Both knew the reason for their anxiety, and both knew quite well that in their case there was only one way to resolve the problem. True, in such a situation it makes it easier to seek the moral support of a psychiatrist, but with a little determination and self-discipline the matter could have been resolved quite easily by the patients themselves. In saying this I do not intend in any way to discourage people from seeking the help of a psychiatrist. The point I wish to make is that in many cases the significant conflict is really quite superficial and well within the capacity of the patient to resolve it, if he will only make a serious attempt to make his behavior agree with his values.

On the other hand many patients are disturbed by conflicts that are deeply unconscious and thus quite inaccessible to the patient. However, it is well for the reader to know that those disturbed by deeply unconscious conflicts form only a minority of the patients coming to consultation in ordinary psychiatric practice.

I now come to the most important observation about psy-

chological conflicts. It is this: that it is simply not necessary
that all our conflicts should be resolved by discussion for
us to obtain peace of mind and function as mature individuals. Psychotherapy in general and psychoanalysis in
particular have become such a vogue of our present culture
that many people lose sight of this simple fact. When all
is said and done, psychoanalysis by its very nature is an
artificial procedure. It can be helpful, but its easy access
may make us forget that man in the process of evolution has
developed within himself a mechanism for dealing with
excessive anxiety and pain. It is to the reawakening of this
mechanism that I would have you turn, rather than to the
endless search for the unconscious conflicts of childhood.

Reducing the Anxiety. We have seen that if we really understand the basic cause of our pain, we do something to
reduce our anxiety and so lessen the pain. Further, if the
cause of our anxiety lies in some conflict that we are aware
of, then we can reduce our anxiety and pain by facing
up to the problem realistically. However, as we now know
there is another way to reduce our anxiety, and that is by
learning how to be more relaxed. We do this by means of
our relaxing mental exercises. While we are practicing them
we are more relaxed. Some of this relaxation stays with us
afterward. Then with continued practice we find it pervad-
ing our everyday life. There is less anxiety in us to motivate
functional pain, and we find that it gradually disappears.

Increasing Our Threshold of Pain. If we gently pinch our
skin, we feel it but it does not hurt us. If we pinch it
harder we come to the stage when it does hurt. This is
our threshold of pain in these particular circumstances. We
can see that our threshold of pain is quite a variable affair.
If we get someone else to pinch us, and at the same time
if we ourselves consciously relax, he is able to pinch much
harder before we feel pain. In a similar way if he distracts

our attention as he pinches us, we do not feel the pain of it so readily. But if our friend makes rather a show of what he is going to do, pain comes more readily because he has mobilized our anxiety, and this lowers our pain threshold.

Our relaxing mental exercises are used to increase our pain threshold in two ways. In the first place the reduction of our general level of anxiety makes us less sensitive to pain, and in the second place we can use our relaxing mental exercises in a positive way to condition ourselves against being disturbed by painful stimuli. It is important to remember that this approach is effective with pain which is due to either functional or organic causes.

THE PSYCHOLOGICAL APPROACH TO PAIN OF ORGANIC ORIGIN

Different people approach pain in different ways. This is largely determined by the personality of the individual, so that we come to fall into some particular attitude toward our pain without giving the matter any real consideration.

We shall discuss these different approaches because this will give us better understanding of the whole problem. It will be seen that each approach has some merit and some disadvantages. You will be able to see which method you yourself are unconsciously using, and you will be better able to assess its strong points and its dangers.

Enduring the Pain. One can simply endure the pain. There is an absence of psychological reaction. "The pain is there. I have got it. That is all there is to it." This is an attitude of a rather stoic and well-integrated personality.

The disadvantage of such an approach is that nothing is done to alleviate the pain. The individual merely endures it, suffers it, and puts up with it as best he can.

The advantages are rather on the negative side. Inasmuch as there is no reaction, no distress, no guilt or fear, the pain is not made worse by any untoward response on the part of the sufferer.

Denial of the Pain. In many areas denial is quite a good way of psychologically protecting ourselves. If we are confronted with some danger that we cannot avoid, it helps us to face the situation if we deny that it is dangerous. In order to convince ourselves we start by denying it to those about us. This makes it easier to deny it to ourselves, and we feel reassured.

Denial can be used in a similar way in an attempt to ease our pain. To the inquiry of our friends we answer, "No, it is not hurting at all." This has two effects. In the first place it makes it easier to deny the pain to ourselves; and secondly there is a kind of primitive magic about it, the magic of saying something to make it come true. Children in their play evoke this kind of magic, and severe pain often has the effect of making us regress, so that we tend to behave in a rather childish way. Among adults we see an example of the same magic of words when someone refuses to say something bad about a friend in jest lest it come true.

Denial helps us to control our pain to some extent, but it is seldom complete. However, there is a quite important side issue. As long as we attempt to deny our pain, whether successfully or not, we at least hold off the destructive influences of distress, fear, and guilt.

Distraction of Attention. If our attention can be distracted we obtain respite from our pain. It would seem that our mind can only hold one topic in consciousness at a time. If our attention can be diverted away from our pain onto some other matter, then we are no longer conscious of our pain. A child falls and hurts himself. He cries with pain. Mother picks him up, and looking out the window says, "Oh, I thought I saw a rabbit under that bush." The pain ceases. If his attention is diverted only momentarily his pain returns. But if his mother can maintain his attention for a few moments, while the painful stimuli settle down, then there is no return of the pain.

The same thing happens with us adults. The patient with arthritis says, "I am better when I am doing something. I am really better at work; the pain does not worry me so much then." We often make conscious efforts to divert our attention from our pain by going to a show, watching TV or by conversation with our friends. The difficulty, of course, is that our brain gives a very high priority for attention to pain of any severity. It therefore usually requires something of real urgency to divert our attention. This is seen in soldiers wounded in battle who continue to fight with little awareness of their wound. In a similar way injured football players often finish the game before they are fully aware of the extent of their injury.

Bearing Pain by Expiation. We have considered the way in which pain is associated with punishment, and how it may cause us to ponder our misdeeds of the past. We may come to feel that we are deserving of punishment. This pain is punishing us now. The sooner the punishment is over the better.

This state of mind, which is not altogether uncommon, may increase our feeling of pain, but at the same time it helps us to endure it.

But remember that this is a pathological sequence of thought which is engendered by the psychological mechanisms which we have already discussed. If you find yourself thinking along these lines, concentrate on this. Yes, you have done wrong. We all have. And now you are suffering from pain. The pain has a real cause whether it be organic or psychological, and is in no way punishment for past misdeeds.

The Masochistic Embellishment of Pain. Just as pain can become associated with the idea of punishment, it can also become associated with the feeling of pleasure. This rather complicated psychological reaction has its origin in sexual experience. The man is active. He is vigorous. His movements are forceful and may cause pain. Thus the ideas of sexual pleasure and causing pain may become associated. This is known as sadism. On the other hand, woman is passive. He does it to her, perhaps forcefully; and feelings of sexual pleasure are intermingled with pain. In these circumstances the pain itself may become tinged with pleasure. This is known as masochism. By various complex psychological reactions either man or woman may become sadistic or masochistic, and the feeling of pleasure in giving or receiving pain may be transferred from sexual experience to the ordinary affairs of everyday life.

However, it is masochism, or the feeling of pleasure involved in experiencing pain, which concerns us in our present discussion. We could find many simple examples of this. When we scratch ourselves perhaps we get a strange feeling of pleasure as we actually injure the skin. There is often a great temptation to pick at a scab on a healing wound. As we pick it, there is a feeling of it hurting, but at the same time there is a pleasurable sensation. People often toy with a little piece of loose skin at the base of a fingernail in much the same way. Many people who discipline themselves very sternly are masochistic. This sometimes applies to those who swim every morning in winter, finding pleasure in the extreme cold. These examples merely serve to show that minor degrees of masochism are accepted as normal behavior.

Under some circumstances this same psychological mechanism of masochism can become stimulated and applied to pain of either functional or organic origin. In a perverse way the pain becomes tinged with a pleasurable feeling. This helps the sufferer to tolerate his pain, or if the condition is more fully developed he may really grow to enjoy the pain. However much this may help the individual to cope with his pain, we must remember that such a process is a gross perversion of the normal senses, and if allowed to develop to meet some particularly painful situation it is likely to lead to complications in other aspects of life.

The Relief of Pain by Autosuggestion. We have already discussed something of the nature of suggestion, noting that it is really a primitive process by which ideas can be accepted into the mind without any critical evaluation. When we offer the ideas ourselves for acceptance by ourselves, the process is known as autosuggestion. In our relaxing mental exercises we use autosuggestion indirectly to reduce our anxiety; but in distinction to this, autosuggestion can be used in the direct control of pain. The process is easier if the suggestion is done by another person, but it can be done by ourselves. It is more efficient if it is used in conjunction with hypnosis, but it can be used quite effectively in the relaxed state obtained in our exercises.

The French physician Emile Coué popularized this approach to the self-management of nervous illness. He first gave the patient exercises to increase his suggestibility. Then he advised that every night on going to bed and every morning before arising the patient should repeat fifteen or twenty times the phrase, "Day by day, in every way, I get better and better." For a while this approach was quite a popular vogue, but it now attracts little interest from either doctors or laymen. Nevertheless, autosuggestion remains quite a useful technique in the self-management of pain. The main reason for its present loss of favor is that the way in which Coué presented the matter is not really suitable for present-day patients.

We often use autosuggestion quite naturally without realizing exactly what we are doing. We make ourselves think, "I am a little better this morning." Sometimes we actually say this to ourselves. In a way we do this so as to stop ourselves thinking anything to the contrary. "The pain is

better. Yesterday it was quite bad, but today it is not too
bad at all."

This all helps, but we can use autosuggestion more effectively if we combine it with our relaxing mental exercises. We go over these ideas in our mind when we are very
relaxed. We do it naturally and easily. We do not just keep
repeating the same sentence, as Coué advised, as this soon
becomes irritating and meaningless. It is important that as
we think the thought, we really know it to be true. If we
say, "I am a little better," we must in fact bring ourselves
to feel a little better as we say it. It is important that we
are very relaxed when we do it, as suggestion and autosuggestion both work much more effectively when we are
relaxed and regressed.

Relief of Pain by Dissociation. Under normal circumstances
there is a wholeness about the individual. The body and
the mind work as a whole. The different parts of our body
and the different aspects of our mind all function in harmony. But in certain conditions this harmony in the working
of the different parts of the body may become disrupted.
This is what we call dissociation. One part or one function
may become dissociated from the rest of the body. Dissociation occurs particularly in hysteria and in hypnosis.

Dissociation can be used in the control of pain. A person
may be hypnotized and his arm may be made quite numb
so that there is no feeling in it whatsoever. In these circumstances sensation in the arm has become dissociated
from the rest of the body. The individual can tolerate any
degree of injury to his arm without feeling the slightest
discomfort. For practical purposes his arm does not belong
to him. Some people can learn to do this themselves by
first inducing an autohypnotic state. Others can produce a
similar effect by consciously dissociating themselves from
the pain or the painful part. If it is a leg that is injured,
we hold ourselves apart from it as it were, and we develop

the feeling that the painful leg really does not belong to us.

It is easy to see how this works for an arm or a leg, but it can also be used for pain in the abdomen, or the chest, or even the head. We develop the feeling that this pain does not really belong to us. We are dissociated from it. It has nothing to do with us. We can stand off as it were, and think about the pain as if in fact it were some other person who were suffering.

People vary a great deal in their ability to use dissociation to control pain. It is much easier to use in the relaxed state of mind that we attain in our relaxing mental exercises. For those who can do it, it is a very good way for the self-management of excessive pain. But it would be wise to confine the use of dissociation to this purpose. It is just possible that unwise experiments in dissociation could lead a very susceptible person into a state in which he might dissociate inadvertently, from having developed a too great facility in the technique, and so produce other symptoms either of his body or mind.

Feeling Pain in Its Pure Form. There is yet another psychological method of coping with pain, and I believe this is the best of all. It is not as complete as psychological dissociation, but it is completely free from the possible dangers which may result from the too facile use of dissociation. In this method we do not try to deny the pain, or make the part concerned numb, or stand apart from the pain. We accept it for what it is—a warning. But we accept it in its pure form without any overlay or embellishment at all. We allow ourselves to experience pure pain, simple and unadorned. When we do this we soon learn that pain—that is, pure pain—really does not hurt at all.

I have warned you several times that your success or failure with this method depends very much on your willingness to go along with me. The idea of pain in pure form not hurting is probably quite new to you. It seems strange. More than that, most likely it seems downright silly. But do not just reject the idea because of this. You have the evidence of my own personal experience and that of many patients. So let yourself go along with me.

The wise use of autosuggestion is very valuable, but the relief of pain by this method is often difficult. For it to be effective we may have to set out deliberately to increase our suggestibility. It is possible that this could have side-effects in the direction of increasing our suggestibility in other areas. These are the problems of the use of autosuggestion in the self-management of pain. Then if we consider dissociation, we see that it is essentially a disintegrating process of the mind, whereas our ultimate goal is complete integration and maturity, which of course is a manifestation of integration. A very significant point about the self-management of pain by feeling pain in its pure form is that it is essentially an integrative process. Therefore the side-effects of learning the self-management of pain in this fashion are all to the good, and work for greater integration and maturity of the personality.

VI

THE SELF-MANAGEMENT OF PAIN

THE PRINCIPLES OF THE SELF-MANAGEMENT OF PAIN
Let us bring together in concise form some of the matters which we have already discussed. You will then be quite clear in your mind as to what the self-management of pain involves. You will see that there are six general principles and that success requires some attention to each of these. You will also see that the application of each of these principles is easy enough to master if you will just let yourself go along with the idea of it.

Reduction of the General Level of Anxiety. This is the first principle in the self-management of pain. It is essential, as anxiety increases pain. The reduction of anxiety is achieved by our understanding the nature of pain, by our facing up to and resolving conflicts which have been causing anxiety, and by the practice of relaxing mental exercises.

The Avoidance of Psychological Reactions That Increase Pain. This principle means that, whatever happens, we shall not allow ourselves to be overwhelmed by distress which is so easily induced by pain. We shall be realistic if the pain should lead us into guilty thoughts about our past shortcomings. By our attitude of mind we shall halt the feeling of fear which would only make us feel our pain more acutely. In each of these matters we gain further help by the calm engendered by the relaxing mental exercises.

The Use of Psychological Reactions That Reduce Pain.
According to circumstances, and according to our own individual personality, at different times we can use various psychological reactions to reduce our pain. We can do what we can to deny it, and use various distractions to forget it. If our personality is such that we can do it, we can dissociate ourselves from the pain and stand apart from it or even make the painful part numb. We can all practice autosuggestion, and most of us can get some help from it provided we do it in a really relaxed state of mind.

The Practice of Relaxing Mental Exercises. This of course forms the basis of this approach to the management of pain. It allays anxiety, wards off distress, allows the effective use of autosuggestion, and of itself reduces our threshold of pain.

Any system that is successful in the self-management of pain is based on a calm and relaxed state of mind. The system described here is simple and effective, and can be mastered by almost anyone who sets his mind to it.

Conditioning Against Pain. Conditioning becomes possible through the calm state of mind induced by the exercises. We subject ourselves to minor painful stimuli. We are not disturbed. Gradually we use more severe stimuli; we maintain our calm of mind and we are still not disturbed. In a little while we can tolerate quite severe stimuli without discomfort. By the process of conditioning, we come to be less disturbed by pain in general. This is possible only by virtue of our relaxed and regressed state of mind while we are doing the conditioning.

The Acceptance of Pain in Pure Form. This is the last of our six principles in the self-management of pain. You may find it more difficult than the others to understand. Actually it follows quite naturally from the practice of the other principles. If you have too much difficulty in believing that pure pain—that is, pain devoid of any psychological reaction—does not really hurt, then concentrate on the other principles which you can understand more easily. Then, when you have mastered them, you will come to realize of your own initiative the fundamental truth of this last proposition—that pure pain does not hurt.

EXERCISES IN DISCOMFORT

Mental Exercises for the Relief of Pain. We proceed with the relaxing mental exercises in exactly the same way as I have described for the relief of anxiety. The only difference is that in the case of pain we have to go a little further, but the principles are just the same. For instance, in discussing phobic anxiety we saw the importance of gradually testing ourselves in the phobic situation. If our phobia concerned going into shops, we went into shops, little by little, easily and naturally, and all the time we concentrated on keeping our calm and relaxed state of mind. We follow the same procedure in dealing with pain.

In doing this there is one point which we must be clear about. The idea of testing out our reaction in the phobic situation by going into the shop seems to us a perfectly natural and common-sense thing to do. But when we come to testing ourselves with pain, we are likely to feel complicated about it. We would rather avoid it as something unnatural and not quite nice. We must not do this. It is just as natural and sensible to test ourselves with pain as it is with anxiety; and it is a very important step in overcoming our pain, just as it was with phobic anxiety.

The first step is learning how to do the relaxing mental exercises which we discussed in relation to anxiety. This is not difficult. We let our bodies relax; we feel the calm that goes with it; we feel it all through us, in our body, in our mind; we let ourselves go; we let go and we drift; we drift in the calm of it, the natural calm and ease that is all through us. We practice this until we can do it quite easily and naturally. Then we do it in increasingly uncomfortable situations. This is the beginning of our use of the relaxing mental exercises in the direct control of pain.

Self-Discipline. This is a difficult subject and because it is difficult it is largely omitted by those who write on these matters. It is obvious that the practice of the exercises and the gradual testing of ourselves with pain requires some degree of self-discipline. But this experience need not be difficult or unpleasant. One of the problems is that we tend to feel embarrassed about the very idea of self-discipline. For instance, it is more than probable that you yourself reacted in some minor way when you read the heading "Self-Discipline" at the beginning of the paragraph. "I know enough about that sort of thing." "This is not the kind of help that I am looking for." "It is easy for those who have no pain to talk about self-discipline for others." Yes, we do react to the idea of self-discipline.

In regard to the last comment, I must say that in my own personal experience I found no great demand on my self-discipline in having my teeth extracted without anesthetic, and many of my patients who have been relieved of pain by this approach are not particularly well-disciplined people in their ordinary life, but were still able to achieve good results.

As the idea of self-discipline is something quite worrying to many people, we shall discuss the matter in some detail. There is a particular necessity for this because of the unrealistic approach of many psychiatrists. In their attempts to bring patients to a freer experience of their emotions, they either directly or indirectly encourage greater freedom of behavior. In getting rid of the inhibitions there is a purposeful relaxing of inner control. This, of course, is the opposite of self-discipline, and it is easy to find evidence that many psychiatrists have gone too far in this direction, so that patients are freed of their inhibitions only to find equal or more severe problems elsewhere.

There are quite different ways of looking at self-discipline. There is the type of self-discipline taught in Sunday school, which is moralistic in the sense that one should discipline oneself against the temptations of evil. Then there is the person who is self-disciplined due to his highly developed sense of duty. The person who is inhibited is often self-disciplined simply because he lacks the emotional freedom to be anything else. The rigid person who is fixed in his ways has a different type of self-discipline which is really a kind of psychological defense. The man who knows what is good for him, and who neither smokes nor drinks, has still another type of self-discipline. By and large these are protective patterns of reaction which work unconsciously to fulfill needs of the individual personality.

The type of self-discipline which I have in mind as necessary for the self-management of pain is something different. It is something much freer, easier, more natural, and much less rigid. People are inclined to think of self-discipline as something rigid; and when it is, it necessarily limits the full potentialities of the personality.

At other times we think of self-discipline as a never-ending struggle—something that is unpleasant, and something we would willingly avoid if we could—something we do not even like to talk about. Again, this is very far from what I have in mind. The self-discipline of the mature person comes easily, naturally, and without effort. Maybe we are not all very mature. But this particular attitude of mind, and that is all that it is, can be developed easily enough.

We know what we want. We want to ease our pain. So we do certain things to accomplish this. There is no problem about it, no conflict, no struggle. We just do it because it is the thing we are going to do.

Discomfort and Relaxation. In order to condition our mind
to be less disturbed by pain, we are deliberately going to
expose ourselves to some degree of discomfort; at the same
time we shall keep our mind calm and relaxed so that the
discomfort simply does not disturb us. And because it does
not disturb us, we do not really perceive it as discomfort at
all.

You suffer from pain. And I suggest to you that you
expose yourself to further discomfort. I can see your reaction.
"No, I have enough suffering. I don't want any more. I
could not bear any more." This reaction is understandable.
But just remember two things. You will not experience any
feeling of discomfort; you will merely place yourself in a
situation which under ordinary circumstances would be uncomfortable, but because of your relaxed state of mind, you
do not feel as uncomfortable. And, secondly, remember that
this is an important step in the self-management of pain,
just as exposure to the phobic situation was in the relief of
phobic anxiety.

Experiments in Discomfort. We must approach the experiments in the right attitude of mind. To condition ourselves
about pain is something quite natural and sensible. There
is no occasion at all for us to feel strange or awkward about
it in any way. We just continue naturally and easily as we
have in the relaxing exercises.

There are two important principles to which we must
always adhere. We must always have ourselves absolutely
relaxed and calm in our mind before we start. If for some
reason we are unable to attain calm and relaxation, we do
not go on with it, but wait awhile until the relaxation comes.
And secondly, in order that our mind can adjust to it, our
exposure to discomfort must be a very gradual process, so
that at no time do we ever become disturbed by it.

The first steps can be lying on a hard surface such as the

floor instead of on a couch, or sitting on a hard chair instead of an armchair.

Before we start on any experiment in discomfort, we always practice for a few moments under comfortable conditions so as first to develop the relaxed state of mind.

When we have mastered one uncomfortable situation, we gradually proceed to more uncomfortable situations, such as lying on a hard surface with pebbles under our back, or putting a clip on a fold of our skin to pinch it. The important thing is that we always maintain our relaxation during the experiment, and we proceed slowly so that we never really get disturbed by the discomfort.

If we should find that the discomfort is breaking through, as it were, so that it is beginning to trouble us, we must not just stop the experiment. Rather, we must relax more deeply, and the tendency for the discomfort to break into our consciousness will pass. Then, and only then, when we have got things quite under control again, do we stop the experiment.

EXERCISES IN PAIN

The Rationale of Exercises in Pain. You may say, "I already suffer enough pain. What good can it do to inflict more pain?" I have asked you to go along with me in these ideas, and I must ask you to go along with me in this. Yes, you are suffering pain. In suffering pain in the way that you do, you are having an experience of suffering uncontrolled pain, pain that you can do nothing about. Perhaps it is better to say that your mind is having an experience of pain which it can do nothing about. Now, what I want to do is to give your mind a different kind of experience—an experience of pain which it càn do something about, of pain which it can control. This new experience will give your mind a basis from which to work. In this first experiment it does not matter if the pain is very slight. The thing that matters is the new experience of the mind in being able to control it.

Difficulties in Exercises with Pain. Exercises for the physical fitness of the body are quite the fashion. But to many people the idea of exercises for the relaxation of the mind seems rather queer, and is only just acceptable. And now we come to pain; and we find the idea of exercises with pain is so strange to most people that they can hardly accept it at all. But it is not simply because the idea of exercises with pain is unusual to people that they are reluctant to accept it. There is something more involved.

As in matters of sex, there is a kind of taboo about pain. And as with sex, there is a reason for the taboo. In discussing the masochistic embellishment of pain, I said something of the nature and origin of sadism and masochism. The idea of the experience of sexual pleasure in the giving or receiving of pain is horrible, and shocks us. It would seem that the taboo against any voluntary experience of pain is in fact a protective mechanism against the activation of the sadomasochistic traits that lie buried within us. Because of the unconscious operation of the taboo, people are loath to experiment with pain, and if they do, they are often faced with misunderstanding by their professional colleagues in much the same way as those who first started to write about sex.

In addition to the problem of the taboo, there are considerable practical difficulties. Experiments with pain involve us in the sensation of pain, which we do not like because it hurts us. Then there is the further difficulty of getting a suitable painful stimulus which does not cause too much bodily injury. Electric shocks are now widely used for this purpose as there is no injury to the tissue. However, this is a biologically unnatural stimulus, as in our evolutionary development we have had no experience of this kind of pain. I have therefore preferred to keep to the simpler and more natural modes of painful stimulus.

Inflicting Pain on Oneself. There is no doubt that these exercises in pain would be easier if I were there to inflict the painful stimulus on you for the first time, rather than you having to do it to yourself. But if you will just make a start, you will find that you can do it quite easily.

Instead of inflicting the pain on the patient, I sometimes do it to myself while the patient is watching, and then ask him to do it to himself. So now, although I am not there with you, you can let yourself feel that I have just done it, quite easily and naturally. I was completely relaxed. There was nothing complicated about it. Now it is your turn.

Experiments with Pinpricks. This is a simple and direct way of providing a painful stimulus of minor degree.

You may suddenly feel, "But I could not stick a pin into myself. The very thought of it upsets me." If you should feel like this, just remember how many diabetics must have said these words. Then after the first few trials they forget all about it, and go on to give themselves their injections naturally and with very little discomfort. You may say, "But the diabetic has to learn this. I don't." But you do. You do, if you wish to master the pain. And there is the evidence of thousands of diabetics that it is really very easy to learn.

Roll up the sleeve on your left arm so as to expose the forearm. Take a pin in your right hand. Now, before you do anything else, let yourself relax. Take your time about it and do it properly. Feel the relaxation of your body, and your face.—Feel the calm.—Let yourself drift.—Your eyes are half open.—You see your forearm, and you see the point of the pin on the skin.—It pushes the skin into a little fold.—You withdraw the pin.

In a way you feel surprised that nothing happened, that there was really no sensation at all. You are utterly relaxed; you feel it in your face and in your mind.—You see the point of the pin on the skin again.—It again pushes the skin into a fold.—There is still no discomfort.—You withdraw the pin.—You are still utterly relaxed.—You do it again.—The pin makes the fold in the skin.—You are utterly relaxed.—You push the pin harder.—It has stuck in the skin.—You leave it there.—You look at the pin sticking in the skin.—The relaxation is still all through you.—You take out the pin.

This is all very simple. But because it is so simple, do not fail to do it. Again, because it is so simple, do not just stick the pin into your arm. Anyone can stick a pin in their skin. Remember that you are doing a particular exercise for a particular purpose. If you take short cuts, the whole point of it is lost. The essential feature of the exercise is keeping the mental relaxation while you are doing it.

In this first experiment, it is a help to let the point of the pin rest on the skin for a moment before pushing the skin into a fold with the pin. By doing it slowly and gently at first, we give our mind time to adjust to the situation, and it also makes it much easier for us to maintain our relaxed state.

Do not try to go too quickly. Aim to be leisurely and natural about it. Spread the experiments over a few days, doing a little more on each occasion.

When we have practiced this a little, we can push the pin into the skin much more firmly, still without causing discomfort.

We can now modify the experiment by jabbing our skin with the pin instead of gently pushing it into the skin. The jabbing is a much more sudden stimulus, and it does not give our mind the extra time to adjust as when we push the pin in slowly. We are very relaxed, completely relaxed, our face and our mind.—We take the pin and make little jabs at the skin, just little jabs at first.—We are so relaxed that our eyes are only half open.—We see the pin jabbing our skin.—There is no discomfort.—We are very, very relaxed.—We jab a little harder.—The pin now sticks in the skin.—We leave it there.—We look at it.—Then we take it out.

Exercises with More Severe Pain. I have mentioned the difficulty of finding a suitable stimulus which produces pain without too much injury to the tissues. I have avoided electric shock as this is not a natural stimulus in the biological sense. After considerable experimentation I have concluded that burning the skin with the glowing end of a thin piece of string is the most convenient stimulus for severe pain. There are different qualities of string, and they vary in the way that they burn. Select the type of string that burns slowly with the end glowing red hot, but without any actual flame. It is desirable to use as thin a string as possible as this provides an adequate stimulus without causing too much blistering. String is often made from winding together three or four thinner strands. If the string is unraveled, one of these thin strands is very suitable.

We expose our forearm. We light the string and have it glowing red.—We relax completely.—With our eyes only half open we see our forearm, and we see the glowing end of the string.—We are very relaxed.—We see the glowing end moving about over our skin.—If there is hair on our arm, we soon smell it burning.—We are very, very relaxed.— For a moment the glowing end touches the skin.—We feel it touch the skin, but it does not disturb us.—We rest.—We relax again, and repeat the experiment. In general it is easiest to do it on an area where there are not many hairs.

Next day there are little blisters on our forearm.

I must warn you again. Do not say that this is something that you could not do. This is not so. Each step follows easily on the previous one. This follows easily on the experiment with pinpricks. Do not say that this is something that you would not wish to do—that there is something wrong about willfully injuring your body. Remember that we have to injure the body in many ways to promote healing. We cut the skin to open an abscess. Many drugs act by injuring the tissue of certain organs and thus reducing their output.

So in the present case, we injure the skin in order to promote the relief of pain.

The experiment with the glowing string can be done in another way. The string is placed on our forearm, and is held in place by resting a fairly heavy metal object, such as an ash tray, on top of it. About two or three inches of string are left protruding from the edge of the metal object. When the end of the protruding string is lighted, it burns down to where it emerges from the edge of the metal object. It then goes out. But at this point it is in firm contact with the skin, and thus provides quite a strong painful stimulus. It is wise at first to be sure that the string projects upward, and does not lie in contact with the skin, or the pain will be too prolonged for a first experiment. This is a good experiment because it creates the feeling that we no longer have control over the painful stimulus. Once we light the string we have to wait until it goes out of its own accord. Until it goes out, we have to control the pain by the depth of our own relaxation. In this way there is a much closer resemblance to pain as it occurs in ordinary life.

When we find that we can do these experiments easily and naturally and without discomfort, we can make another modification. We bend the string so that it lies on our bare skin for a little way before coming to the edge of the metal object which keeps it on our arm. At first try it with the string lying on the skin for only an eighth of an inch. Then when you have done this, have it lie on the skin for greater distances, up to half an inch or longer.

In the early experiments be sure that you use as thin a strand of string as will burn evenly by glowing. Later on, slightly thicker string can be used and the stimulus will be more severe.

The Integration of the Experiments with Everyday Life.
When we were discussing anxiety we were careful to bring the relaxing exercises into relationship with our ordinary

way of living. We found that we could keep the same relaxed state of mind when we were walking along and doing
simple tasks. By this means the calm and ease of the exercises came to pervade all aspects of our life. Now we follow
the same principles in relation to pain.

We have learned to do the exercises with pinpricks and
the burning string in the calm and relaxed state of mind
that we have learned to induce in ourselves. Now we practice
the same exercises in our normal everyday state of calm
and relaxation, without any of the regression which goes
with the mental exercises. We learn to do this gradually.
First we do the pinpricks exercise in deep relaxation; then
we do it with ourselves still relaxed, but less regressed. We
are more alert; our eyes are more widely open, and we are
much more aware of our surroundings and what is going
on. By doing this gradually we find that these stimuli, which
at one time would have been quite painful, now cause us
no discomfort. In other words, our threshold of pain has
been raised. When we can do this with pinpricks, we proceed to practice in the same way with the burning string.

We are now bringing the effect of the exercises into
our everyday life. We find that minor incidents which in
the past would have caused us pain or discomfort are now
no worry to us at all. When such incidents arise, we are
less easily disturbed because of our increased tolerance of
pain, and if the stimulus is sufficiently severe that we find
we are on the verge of pain, we quickly relax in the way
that we have learned, and the threat of pain passes off.

Experiencing Pain in Pure Form. We are now in a better
position to discuss this idea. We can relax and stick a pin
into our skin without feeling discomfort, and we can touch
our skin with the burning string as it glows red hot without
any real feeling of hurt. In both instances we feel something,
as we have not made our arm numb by dissociation. I find

it very hard to describe what we do actually feel. There do not seem to be the right words to describe it. This is so because it is a feeling which we do not ordinarily experience. It is not just the feeling of touch because there is more in it than that. It is not pain as we ordinarily know it because it does not hurt. It is in fact the feeling of pure pain.

As we learn to do our exercises with less and less regression, we become more fully aware of this new sensation. It is not a nice sensation, neither is it nasty. There is no pleasure in it as in the masochistic embellishment of pain. We can feel pleased in a natural way with our newly learned ability to experience pain in this fashion, but this is a reality-based pleasure and quite distinct from the perverted pleasure of masochism.

As with the other aspects of this system of self-management of anxiety and pain, we integrate this principle into our ordinary way of life. When by chance we are exposed to pain, we recollect the sensation of pure pain which we experienced during our exercises, and as we relax, the present pain merges into this new sensation. We must practice this in all the incidents of trivial pain which befall us. In the past we have borne these minor incidents just as best we could; but now we use them to practice our new-found ability.

THE SELF-MANAGEMENT OF DIFFERENT KINDS OF PAIN

The Prevention of Pain When We Are Expecting It. One of the difficulties when we are expecting something painful to happen to us is that we tend to become anxious. Our anxiety shows itself in tension of both body and mind, and as a result we feel the pain more intensely. This commonly happens with children when they are given an injection. It also happens with adults on such occasions as when a boil is lanced or when they are subjected to painful examination by medical instruments.

But now that we have practiced our relaxing mental exercises the situation is quite different. When we know that something painful is going to happen to us, we simply relax. This not only prevents the pain being made worse by anxiety, but allows us to experience the pain in pure form so that we are not distressed or hurt by it. In general, pain that we are able to anticipate is quite easy to control by this system of self-management.

A dentist phoned me, and with rather a laugh in his voice explained that he had known a nineteen-year-old student for more than nine years and was simply unable to get near him to do some urgent dental work. Could I help?

There is no other way to describe him: the poor boy was simply a terrible coward. This had been the pattern all his life. Although a big boy, at school he had avoided all games for fear of getting hurt. Apparently the dentist had been very patient and had tried to coax him along little by little. But it was all no good. He had a mouth full of carious teeth, but he could not stand the thought of being given an injection or having a tooth touched with the drill.

I showed him how to relax—very slowly, as he was even frightened of this. I then brought him to tolerate the minor discomfort of having him relax on the couch with a prickly metal object under his shoulders. Still progressing very slowly, I tested him with pinpricks, and later with a clip on his skin. He was then sent back to the dentist, who subsequently reported that he had been able to do his work without undue trouble.

The Self-Management of Chronic Pain. This involves the understanding and practice of the various ideas which we have discussed. Remember that this is not difficult, but it requires a little time and a little perseverance. Remember that many patients whom I have told these things verbally have succeeded. The only difference with you is that I am telling you by writing it down instead of saying it in words; and actually by writing it down I am able to explain it much more fully.

We have spoken of six general principles in the self-management of pain. If you were with me in my consulting room, I would repeat them to you in order to impress them on your mind. So I shall do the same now.

1. Reduce your general level of anxiety by understanding the nature of pain, by facing and resolving conflicts which cause anxiety, and by using the relaxing mental exercises to reduce anxiety.
2. Guard against the reactions that make pain worse. Do not allow distress, guilt, or fear to take over.
3. Use the reactions that reduce pain. Deny it, and distract yourself from it when you can. Relax deeply and practice autosuggestion. When you can, use dissociation.
4. Practice the relaxing mental exercises.
5. Increase your pain threshold by conditioning yourself with the exercises in discomfort and pain.
6. Learn to experience and accept pain in pure form, which does not hurt.

We have discussed the means of fulfilling each of these principles, and we have seen that each step in itself is not difficult, as one follows the other in ordered gradation.

I always warn my patients of three things: Do not expect too much too quickly. Expect a few ups and downs, good days and bad days in the process of mastering the self-management. Do not get cross with yourself if at first you cannot do just what I ask.

I could relate many examples of patients I have had who have been successful in learning how to control their pain.

A man with cancer of the prostate suffered severe pain from secondary growths in the bones of his pelvis. He learned to relax and control the pain reasonably well, so that the last weeks of his life were actually spent in a clear mind and relative comfort.

A woman in her sixties complained of continuous severe pain in the legs, the vagina, and the area of the bladder. An operation on her back had shown a cystic degeneration of the nerve roots. So there was no doubt about the organic origin of her pain.

At first she found it hard to accept the idea that a psychological approach could help pain of this nature. She kept saying, "But the nerves have this degeneration." I asked her to stick some pins into my forearm. She was reluctant, but she eventually did so, and was obviously surprised that it did not seem to hurt me. I then had her relax, and I did the same to her. When she opened her eyes she was astounded to find a couple of pins well embedded in her skin. From then on she was most enthusiastic about the exercises. She lost all the pain in her legs, and most of it, but not all, in her vagina and bladder. She later stated that she had developed a real peace of mind, and she volunteered that she was sleeping better than she had for eight or nine years.

I well remember one of my first experiments in helping people with organically determined pain. A woman in her sixties suffered chronic pain in her back from a degenerative condition of her backbone. She said that she had to fly from Melbourne to London and back, and she was terrified of the pain from having to remain in one position in her seat for so long. This was before the advent of the jets.

I taught her to relax and wished her luck. A few weeks

later she came in to thank me, saying that she had made the trip without discomfort.

Just a year ago I saw a retired doctor, aged seventy-six years, who had had an extremely painful condition of his foot for nine years. He kept describing it as feeling as if someone were screwing up his foot in a vise. One surgeon had cut the main nerve, another surgeon had dissected the little nerves that lead to the toes, and later the artery had been freed of its nerves. But nothing had any effect on the pain. Another psychiatrist had tried hypnosis, but this was also unsuccessful.

In spite of his age he learned to do the relaxing mental exercises, and soon found he could control the pain.

A few days ago I received a note from his wife saying that he had died, and thanking me for the relief he had had in this last year of his life.

The Self-Management of Sudden Unexpected Pain. This is a different clinical problem again. The difficulty with sudden unexpected pain is that the pain is likely to get out of hand and overwhelm us. It is then easy to be overcome with distress before we can compose ourselves. It happens in the case of an unexpected blow, a broken bone, a burn, or even a severe sprain.

Our studies in the self-management of pain help in two ways. If we have learned something of the approach and have had some experience in the mental exercises, we do not react so drastically to sudden pain. This has been my own experience, and a number of patients have volunteered a similar observation. In the second place, if we should find that we are suddenly threatened with loss of control in this way, we now have the means to bring ourselves quickly under control and restore our composure.

As in each of the other aspects of pain and anxiety, we work to bring our principles of self-management more and more into our everyday life. So when we experience some sudden and unexpected pain, even if it is only of minor degree, we immediately restore our composure by momentary mental relaxation instead of giving vent to our feelings as we have done in the past. Be warned that there is a good deal of false teaching by psychiatrists and those who should know better that it is good to give vent to our emotions and feelings. If we give vent to our feeling of pain, we too easily become distressed, and the intensity of the pain is increased.

Four years ago a dentist came to me. He has a degenerative condition of his backbone so that the nerves are pinched as they come from the spinal cord between the bones. He suffered sudden unexpected twinges of acute pain as well as quite severe chronic pain. His work as a dentist with the long hours on his feet and the necessity of leaning forward over the patient made him very vulnerable to this condition.

He has learned to control the pain. He is still working full-time. Between patients he occasionally lies down in a side room for a few minutes to re-establish his mental and physical relaxation.

A seventy-two-year-old single woman was referred to me in the hope that I might be able to help her with the pain of her *tic douloureux*. This is a shockingly painful condition characterized by sudden jabs of acute pain in the side of the face. The first attack had come on eleven years previously, but this had settled down. She was not subject to continual jabs of pain when she was talking or eating. On occasions the pain was excruciating. Three years previously she had developed trigger points on the face and tongue, and if these were touched, it would precipitate excruciating pain. At night if she moved in her sleep and the bedclothes brushed her face, pain would be precipitated in this way.

She was a very courageous, stoic woman, and I have no doubt that at times she experienced really terrible pain. However, she wanted to avoid the orthodox treatment by injection or the operation of cutting the nerve, both of which leave that part of the face without feeling and so open to injury.

She was a particularly good patient, as are many people who are in extreme pain. I only saw her on four occasions. She then claimed that she could reduce the pain to quite bearable proportions; and she did in fact allow me to touch the trigger spots, which previously had been so exquisitely tender.

The Pain of Childbirth. I do not intend to discuss each and every form of pain, but this system lends itself so well to the control of the pain of childbirth that we must have a few final words about it.

All through this study we have emphasized the disastrous effect of anxiety on pain. The young woman approaching childbirth is in fact subjected to an extraordinary number of anxiety-producing influences. Other women seem bent on telling her stories of terrible pain and complications. The stories often end with a kind of negative suggestion, "But you will be all right, dear," which of course conveys the idea that she just might not be all right. Many women tend to talk of their experience of childbirth in the way that others describe their adventures in sports or war. "Of course, I had to have six stitches." All this has its effect on the young woman. The very fact of going to the hospital makes her feel that there is something wrong. She thus goes with a high level of anxiety to have her baby, and with the clear expectation of suffering considerable pain. Her anxiety not only lowers her threshold of pain, but may tend to make the contractions of the womb less smooth and coordinated. And worst of all, anxiety makes tense those parts which should relax, so that they are painfully forced by pressure instead of relaxing easily and naturally.

However, the young woman can guard against these unpleasant eventualities by being secure in her knowledge that childbirth is a natural process, and that older women often gain some strange satisfaction in telling exaggerated stories of their own experiences.

An unfortunate aspect of the problem is that the situation tends to become self-perpetuating. The woman in her first pregnancy is made anxious and expects pain. As a result, she experiences pain. Then with this experience behind her, she is increasingly nervous at her second pregnancy, and the painful experience is repeated, and so on. One of the reasons why this unhappy state of affairs is allowed to persist is that obstetricians are usually very busy people and often short of sleep. They simply do not spend the necessary time with the expectant mother to put these things right.

In this study we have learned enough about psychological mechanisms to realize that success requires more than a clear and logical statement of the facts. It requires leading the person to know and to understand, which is something quite different.

With these thoughts in mind, do a little preparation for the coming event. Practice the relaxing mental exercises, naturally and easily, so that you can let yourself go into the relaxed mental state when you wish it. This will also help you with the discomfort of the increased weight of the last few weeks. If you like, you can practice the exercises with pain, but this is not essential, because if you really learn the mental relaxation, pain will not be a problem.

When you feel the first contractions—this is what the older women call "the pains"—remember what is happening. The muscles of your womb are contracting to push your baby down into the birth canal. As the contraction comes on, you let yourself go.—You let yourself go completely.—You let yourself go in body and mind as you feel the contraction.—You feel it good and strong.—It is good, pushing the baby down to be born.—It is strong.—You feel the strength, natural strength.—Natural, so that there is no hurt.—Between the contractions you lie back, easy and relaxed.—And all the time you have with you the calm and the relaxation of the mental exercises.

The baby is pushed down the birth canal slowly and easily and naturally. His head comes to the muscles at the end of the canal. You feel this because there are more nerves in these muscles. Now you relax deeper, deeper than ever, knowing that it is good that he has reached the end of the canal, and in a few moments he will be born.

There is just one other point that I would mention. Some people feel that they do not get themselves deep enough, as it were, in their relaxing mental exercises. They feel, "This would not be sufficient if I were in real pain." The fact is that when we are actually faced with potentially painful stimuli, as in childbirth, we can let ourselves go very much more completely. This may seem strange to you, but it is true. The reason is that in practicing our exercises we lack real psychological motivation; we only have an intellectual logical motivation, which is not the same thing. So in the actual situation we surprise ourselves by doing much better than we expected.

Just one last comment. Take your obstetrician into your confidence about what you are doing. Remember that obstetricians have different views about this kind of approach, and that some still adhere to a rather mechanistic, drug-oriented way of doing things. Do not let any conflict develop between you and your doctor on account of this, as such would only cause tension. It is best to find out the obstetrician's views early in pregnancy, so that if necessary you can find another who will go along with you in these matters. If it is too late for this, go along with him. If he wants you to have drugs or injections, do not fight about it. In any case, you will need very much less than if you had not had the experience of the mental exercises.

CONCLUSION

Earlier on I mentioned the fringe benefits which come un-
asked as a result of these relaxing mental exercises. These
were matters that were easy to discuss and record—better
sleep; greater ease at work; less tension in the home;
better sexual response; and improved responses, both mental
and physical, in many other aspects of our life.

But there is something else, something much more elusive,
something much more significant. I have experienced it. I
also know that others have experienced it, although they
have rarely told me so.

You may easily think to yourself, "Well, how does he
know?" I know in the same way as you will know when it
comes to you.

When I was asking him about the nature of meditation,
the yogi saint of Katmandu told me, "You can show a child
a banana, but you cannot tell him how it tastes." Taste the
flavor of your relaxing mental exercises. Taste it deeply.
And you will know what I mean. This that is greater than
all the rest.

I have tried to write as if I were talking with you in
my consulting room. If you were here with me, I would
ask you to drop me a note just to let me know how things
have gone with you.

As a doctor I want to know the result of my treatment.
If the treatment is not quite orthodox, it is all the more
important that we know the result. Please, if you have had

help from this let me know. What was your trouble? How long had you had it? Then these ideas can be put to others with the additional weight of your own experience. Good luck.

Ainslie Meares, M.D.
45 Spring Street,
Melbourne, Australia.

INDEX

Daydreaming, 36, 86

Dependent relationships, 52–54, 55

Depression: from anxiety and nervous tension, 7, 14–16, 129; from nervous illness, 15; as reaction to loss or bereavement, 15–16; and pain, 140–41, 146

Diarrhea, nervous, 5, 25–26, 133

Discomfort, exercises in: mental exercises for relief of pain, 160–61; self-discipline, 161–62; discomfort and relaxation, 163; experiments in discomfort, 163–64

Dissociation, 155–56, 157

Distress, and pain, 128, 135–37, 158

Dreams, quality of, 14

Drifting sensation in regression, 83

Drug addiction, 36

Dysmenorrhea, 31

Dyspepsia, nervous, 24–25

Elderly persons, and exercise for insomnia, 102

Emotional remoteness and too close relationship, 42

Examinations, and student anxiety, 7, 16, 26, 118, 133

Exercises in pain: rationale of, 164; difficulties in, 165; inflicting pain on oneself, 165–66; experiments with pinpricks, 166–67; with more severe pain, 168–69; integration of, with everyday life, 169–70; experiencing pain in pure form, 170–71

External environment as basis for nervous impulses, 3, 7

Eyelids: trembling of, 85; relaxing of, 89–91

Face, relaxation of muscles of, 80, 81, 97

Fatigue of anxiety, 14

Fear: feeling of, 9, 16, 61; of pregnancy, 39; and pain, 141–43, 158. See also Phobias and phobic tension

Freud, Sigmund, 40

Friends, difficulties with, 16–18

Frigidity, 26–27; relaxing exercises as aid in, 112–14

Fringe benefits from self-management of anxiety, 123–24, 180

Frustrations, reaction to, 13–14, 111

"Getting under one's skin," 30

Guilt feelings, 7, 33, 40, 129; and pain, 137–40

Handedness, and stuttering, 21

Headache, nervous, 30, 135

Heart: palpitation of, 22–23; pain in region of, 23–24

Home, insecurity at, 50–51

Homosexuality, 34–35; and relaxing mental exercises, 121

Hypnosis: use of, in asthma, 28; use of autosuggestion in, 154; dissociation in, 155

Ideas: significance of, when mind is regressed, 76; acceptance of, into the mind, 93–94

Impending disaster, feeling of, 11

Impotence, 27–28

Impulses, nervous, 3–4; integration of, 4, 62–63

Inferiority complex, 44